Christianity and Socialism

BY

WASHINGTON GLADDEN

Author of "Who Wrote the Bible?" "Tools and the Man,"
"Social Facts and Forces," "Social Salvation," etc.

**Fredonia Books
Amsterdam, The Netherlands**

Christianity and Socialism

by
Washington Gladden

ISBN: 1-4101-0046-4

Reprinted from the 1905 edition

Fredonia Books
Amsterdam, The Netherlands
http://www.fredoniabooks.com

PREFATORY NOTE

THE title of this little book is not, I fear, very descriptive; but it has something to say about Socialism, and much about Christianity. And I trust that it may help a little to bring the two into more intelligible and more friendly relations.

These five lectures were given, in January, 1905, before the students of Drew Theological Seminary—the second, third, and fourth of them in the Seminary Chapel at Madison, New Jersey, the first and last in New York city. They were not prepared for consecutive delivery, and they are more disconnected and more repetitious than they would have been if thus prepared; but they contain some honest thinking, and some serious endeavors to

reach the fundamental and constructive
ideas of our social life.

I cannot speak too warmly of the cor-
diality with which a Congregationalist was
welcomed in this stronghold of the Meth-
odists, nor of the hospitality extended to
him and to his message. And I wish that
this little book might be a witness to the
unity of the Spirit which is binding our
churches together in the bonds of peace.

WASHINGTON GLADDEN.

Columbus, Ohio, July 10, 1905.

CONTENTS

CONTENTS

Christianity and Socialism

I

The Sermon on the Mount as the Basis of Social Reconstruction

THE Sermon on the Mount has been called the Magna Charta of Christianity. That which is fundamental and distinctive in the teachings of Jesus Christ is supposed to be included in this discourse. Those who believe that the teachings of the Master contain the normative principles of human society are naturally inclined to turn their attention first to this remarkable sermon, which seems to furnish the keynote of his ministry. It should be noted, however, that the social morality of this Teacher is by no means all expressed in this discourse. Important elements of it must be sought in other parts of the gospels. Nevertheless, that which is here set forth is fundamental and far-reaching; doubtless, if we give due attention to what is here, we shall need, like Browning's Pambo, to take several generations to master this before we go on to what is higher.

The subject before us is the basis laid in the Sermon on the Mount for social reconstruction. As a student of social problems I wish to see how much I can find in these three chapters of the first gospel to aid us in repairing or rebuilding modern society.

At the first re-reading, with this thought in mind, of these words which many of us have known by heart from our childhood, it strikes one that social problems do not bulk very large in this exhibit. It is not society, it is the individual to whom these words appear to be addressed. It is not for groups or bodies of men, in their corporate relations, that these counsels are primarily intended, but for persons. And this is true. Primarily these words do apply to the individual. Not to isolated individuals, as we shall see; always to individuals as members of society, but still to individuals. The conscience, the judgment, the will, belong to individuals, and if anything is to be done for society it must be done by the coöperation of individuals. The wise preacher, whether on the mount or on the plain, always preaches to individuals. There is no such thing as a corporate mind that he knows anything of or can intelligently address. There are men and women before him whose state of mind he knows more or less perfectly—this manufacturer, that banker, this teacher, that clerk, this housewife, that mechanic, this man of leisure, that woman of society—and he must fit what he has to say to the intellectual and moral demands of these. Doubtless he recognizes them as types, and hopes to reach many by the word which he aims at one. But it remains true that all skillful teaching deals with individuals, and not with masses. "The one truth that experience and history impress upon us," says Dr. Bascom, "is that the problem of growth is primarily an interior one, and that social progress, therefore, is always gathered up and expressed in personal progress. Nothing will reach that which does not reach this; and nothing which reaches this will fail to extend to that also. The spiritual world is what its spiritual occupants make it to be, and the kingdom of heaven can only come as it comes in the hearts of individuals. And so it becomes a problem of immense labor to carry the individual forward through all the slow stages of growth in concert with other individuals to the point in which strength and wisdom and peace abide in each singly and in all collectively." [1]

There can be no doubt that this truth is greatly neglected at the present time by many students of social problems; and it is well for those of us to whom the words of Christ are words of authority to read over with some care the constitution of the kingdom of heaven as he here outlines it, and see what principles he emphasizes.

The first word touches with a sure stroke one of the great qualities of personal character. "Blessed are the poor in spirit: for theirs is the kingdom of heaven." The kingdom which he comes to found belongs not to the conceited, the self-sufficient, the people who know it all; but to the humble-minded, the modest,

[1] The Words of Christ, p. 3.

those who are conscious of their own defects of knowledge and power, and are willing to receive light and help from others. This spirit of humility, Jesus seems to say, is fundamental in personal character. To be right yourself, rightly to help others, you must begin here. And this is precisely what Bacon said about the spirit of science. The mighty scientific progress of recent centuries is due to the recognition of this fact more than to any other one thing. The method which Bacon suggested is the only right method of scientific study. "If in this high and arduous attempt we have any proficiencie," he says, "surely by no other means have we cleared ourselves a way than by a sincere and just humiliation of the spirit of man to the laws and operations of nature." The same method is not less indispensable in social science than in physical science. It is not the pushing, the egotistic, the opinionated, who are going to give us most help in the solution of these great questions; but those who have knowledge enough to comprehend that they are great questions, and humility enough to bring to their discussion a spirit of teachableness and sweet reasonableness. One who visits the places where such themes are sometimes discussed, and observes the headiness and cocksureness and intolerance of many of those who speak, is made painfully aware of the fact that the kingdom of heaven is yet a great way off. To people of this temper any kind of social machinery ever invented would bring only hell. There is scarcely another condition of social reconstruction more fundamental than this, albeit it concerns the individual alone.

Others of these maxims, on which I must not dwell, deal also with personal character. "Blessed are they that hunger and thirst after righteousness: for they shall be filled" with that for which they hunger and thirst. It is not the man whose chief craving is for comfort or ease or income or equality, but the man who above all things wants to be right in thought and wish and deed, whom this beatitude crowns. That his own life may conform to the law of life, that he may be the man he ought to be, this is his ruling passion. There will never be any good society among men who lack this quality.

"Blessed are the pure in heart: for they shall see God." The beatific vision is not for paradise; it is for these days of toil and turmoil when nothing is so much needed by any of us as to discern the presence of Him whose blessed will, in all these confusions, is slowly unfolding. Only the pure in heart can see God; and no one can help much in building a good society who cannot see him.

Remember also that you are the salt of the earth, the light of the world. But the salt and the light perform their functions not in conventions or by means of resolutions; it is by what they are in themselves that they exercise power, not by what they try to do. The attention is here sharply called to the possession of personal qualities by which alone the man becomes a savor of life and a point of radiation for the whole community.

So, too, bear in mind that the obedience of every law primarily concerns the inward motive, and that both in our worship and in our charity the main test touches the secret impulse. And do not forget that the restless temper which fills the days and nights with worry about what we shall eat and drink and wherewithal we shall be clothed is the bane of life; that the first condition of happiness is to get rid of that. And, above all, remember that a deep and true moral insight, the power of seeing things as they are, the intuitive vision which quickly and keenly discerns between the real and the unreal, the false and the true, is the one thing needful. "If thine eye," the eye of the soul, "be single, thy whole body shall be full of light; but if thine eye be evil, thy whole body shall be full of darkness. If, therefore, the light that is in thee be darkness, how great is that darkness!"

I have only touched on a few of the points which concern our personality which Jesus emphasizes in this discourse. It is evident that his primary concern is with the individual; that he has no confidence in getting a good society out of bad men; that he means to strike home at our personal sins and defects and make us all feel that the place to begin every social reform is in the heart of the reformer. "First cast out the beam that is in thine own eye; and then shalt thou see clearly to cast out the mote out of thy brother's eye." I am persuaded that no more salutary word could be spoken in most assemblies of social reformers than this which Jesus Christ would be sure to speak to them. All of us need to be sharply recalled to the truth that our own motives and principles of action must be pure and right if we would render any valuable service to our fellow men.

The recognition of this fact will show us at once what a task we have before us. Harmonious social relations must result from right purposes and social tempers in individuals; and yet it is true, as Dr. Bascom says, that "conditions of close spiritual relationship hardly exist as yet between any two men. The soul is rather startled in its progress by its own growing solitude. When oppressed with such an experience the wise man does not feel that

he has grounds of complaint, that the
keynote of life is with him, and that others
make the discord. He is rather impressed
with the fact of how extended, difficult,
and complicated a combination is a true
spiritual symphony. How many things in
oneself must be increased, diminished,
modified, eliminated, before he can successfully take part in it; while the same is
true of those about him who are best fitted
to unite their experience with his experience. How little right has anyone to
find fault with these discords; or, if he
assumes the right, how is he carried still
farther off from the desired harmony!"[1]

It is evident that the great Choragus
will have much tuning of the instruments
to do before the music of the spheres will
be reproduced in human society. Nevertheless, that is the glorious result toward
which the whole creation moves, and it is

[1] The Words of Jesus, p. 4.

for us to keep it in view, and patiently to strive toward it. For the perfection set before us, in this great discourse, is a social as well as an individual perfection. Individuals we are, but we are not monads. Our life is forever a related life. We cannot obey, in solitariness, the law of our being. We must take care to be right in ourselves, but we can never be right by ourselves or for ourselves; our humility, our purity, our integrity, our sincerity, our serenity, our insight, are not possessions that we can monopolize; they are the instruments of service. And Jesus brings before us, in this discourse, the fundamental conditions of the perfect society.

Of all these conditions the most fundamental is that which is expressed in the first sentence of the universal prayer, "Our Father who art in heaven."

Let us pause before these well-worn

words; let us speak them reverently.
Here, if Jesus is authority, is the corner
stone on which the whole social structure
rests. Society exists among human beings
by virtue of the fact which these words
convey. The Fatherhood of God gives us
a foundation for social order and peace and
welfare; other foundation can no man lay.

Many indeed have been the attempts
to rest the social structure on other bases,
to find some other theory by which to ex-
plain the existence of the human commonwealth. It has been conceived that
men enter into social relations through
some sort of voluntary compact, because
they think it will be profitable for them
to do so; that society is the result of a kind
of copartnership agreement. And there
are not a few who believe that economic
motives are the primary motives in the
constitution of human society. This is
certainly not the doctrine of the Sermon

on the Mount. Nor does it agree with those facts of human life which are best known to us all.

"Many writers," says Frederick Maurice, "begin with considering mankind as a multitude of units. They ask, 'How did any number of these units form themselves into a society?' I cannot adopt that method. At my birth I am already in a society. I am related, at all events, to a father and mother. This relation is the primary fact of my existence. I can contemplate no other facts apart from it.

"Perhaps you will say, 'For each of us separately that no doubt is true. But we want to consider the world at large.' Well! and to what portion of the world at large is this truth not applicable? In what region do you find a man who is not born a son; who is not related to a father and mother? It is a fact for me, surely; but it is a fact for you and for every man.

And if you determine not to take notice of this fact, not to give it precedence of every other, the effect is that instead of contemplating the world at large, you will only contemplate yourself. *You* will be the unit about which all events and persons will revolve. Each man will regard himself as the center of the universe. You will at last come to an understanding —a very imperfect understanding—that each must occupy his place in his own estimation; you will be forced to construct a society on that hypothesis. If, on the other hand, you start from the indisputable commonplace, 'We are sons,' such a way of considering the universe is from the first impossible. I cannot be the center of the circle in which I find myself, be it as small as it may. I refer myself to another. There is a root below me. There is an Author of my existence.''[1]

[1] Social Morality, pp. 21, 22.

These are the primal facts of human society. We are born into social relations. Existence is a social fact. My conscious life, descending to me by ordinary generation, unites me to my kind, and issues, can only issue, from him who is the Author of all life—of whom every fatherhood in heaven and on earth is named. Every human being has the same parentage. The Father in heaven is the Father of us all.

This fact of fatherhood and sonship, if I recognize it, makes it impossible for me to assume an egoistic or independent attitude. If I have a Father in heaven, he owes to me care, guidance, wise control, and I owe to him reverence, trust, obedience. Thus the very foundation of society is in religion. The first right social act must be an act of worship. And since my very existence is derived and dependent, the spirit of subordination and obedience must be natural to me. I am under authority. There is a superior to whom I owe allegiance. Fatherhood is not tyranny, it never is; and sonship is not bondage. The relation is one of loving care and control—even of self-sacrifice—on the one hand, and of loving trust and honor on the other; but the spirit of obedience is there. No true family is without it.

Thus the recognition of the fact of the universal Fatherhood must fill society with the spirit of docility, of gentleness, of subordination. That is the manner of it, as Maurice says. That is the mental habit which befits it. The individuals of whom it is composed are not independent units, each of whom considers himself the center of the universe; they are children who know themselves to be subject to the loving will of the universal Father, whose purposes concerning them and all the rest of his children are to be the law of their lives.

From the fact of the divine Fatherhood is derived the fact of human brotherhood. What the right relation of brothers must be, when the Fatherhood is divine, it is not easy to tell, though it is not hard to understand. Honor and obedience to the Father will rule all our conduct. We must therefore think his thoughts about our brothers; we must share in his purposes concerning them. The law of sympathy, of consideration, of helpful love, will be the law of all human association. The deepest and most central fact to be considered in all relations with my fellow man—whether he be employer or employee, teacher or pupil, client or customer, neighbor or foreigner—is that he is my brother; that we have a common Father; and that his welfare, his happiness, his honor, his manhood, ought to be as dear to me as my own.

This relation of brotherhood between human beings is the second fundamental social fact, according to the teaching of Jesus. Observe that it is a fact. It is not merely a thing that ought to be; it is the thing that is. It is not true that human beings ought to become brothers; it is true that they are brothers. No choice or determination or wish of theirs can have anything to do with the fact. It is true that a great many human beings do not behave toward each other as if they were brothers, but their bad behavior does not change the fact. The relation is there. It is the deepest thing in our lives. It is the one thing that Jesus came to make plain to us, and to help us to realize. All the human beings that I meet day by day in the street, in the mart, in the shop, in the office, in the drawing-room, in the

kitchen, are the children of my Father. I
owe to them, first of all, a brother's sympathy, a brother's help. The laborer who
works for me, the mechanic at my forge,
the hostler in my stable, the maid in my
house, the shopgirl behind my counter,
are the children of my Father. My constant question concerning them all must be,
not, How much profit can I get out of them?
but, How much good can I do them? The
employer for whom I work, the man who
pays me wages, is my brother. It is my
duty to think of his well-being, to consider
how I may add to his peace and happiness.
The man who lives on the avenue beside
me, the man who lives in the alley in the
rear, are equally my brethren. What can
I add to their well-being? The man of
whom I buy or to whom I sell, of whom I
borrow or to whom I lend, who comes to
me for counsel or to whom I go for service,
the postman on his rounds, the policeman

on his beat, the pauper in the almshouse, the prisoner in the jail, are all my brothers —what can I do to help them, succor them, bless them? All my relations with all these human beings must be inspired and dominated by this central fact of brotherhood. Whatever I do or omit to do with reference to them must be governed by the wish to realize this relation. If ever I forget this, or ignore it, in any social act, I am hindering the coming of that kingdom for which I daily pray.

You may say that all this is visionary and chimerical; that no such relations as these have ever existed or ever will among human beings; that it is worse than useless to suggest a rule of life that is so utterly beyond the powers of man; that society can never be put upon any such basis as this, and that, if we wish to see society reconstructed, we must seek for some theory of human relations somewhat less

quixotic.   To all which I reply that I
am not giving you my theory of human
society.   I am simply trying to state
that theory as I find it laid down by
Jesus Christ in the Sermon on the Mount.
I cannot, for the life of me, make it mean
any less or any other than that which I
have unfolded.   If the Fatherhood of God
and the brotherhood of man mean anything at all, they mean all this.

It is open to any man to say that
Jesus Christ knew nothing about the
proper ordering of social relations; that
while he may be a safe guide for those
who wish to find the way to heaven, he
is not to be trusted as a social philosopher.
And this is practically what is said by a
good many persons in the church as well
as out of it.   Those who are most eager
to affirm his divinity are often most bold
to deny his authority when he speaks of
human relationships and obligations.   For

my own part, I must confess that I cannot
so divide his words; and that his teaching
respecting the divine Fatherhood, with its
corollary, appears to me to be the very
substance of his mission. And the denial
of this is, to my mind, the very *fons et origo*
of all unbeliefs and heresies.

Yet it must be owned that this denial
has been almost universal among those
who have stood to represent Christ on
the earth. The doctrine of the universal
Fatherhood has not been generally ac-
cepted, as Christ taught it, by the Christian church. To those who are under the
wrath and curse of God on account of the
fall, the Fatherhood, we have been told,
ceases to be a fact; it is a possibility
merely. Those who are elect and regenerate may claim it, none others. That is
the received theology. To the regenerate,
all this teaching of Jesus about the Fatherhood and the brotherhood may apply.

The relation between regenerate men may indeed be such as this teaching suggests; but how, it is demanded, can there be an actual brotherhood among the unregenerate, since for them there is no actual Fatherhood? Outside the church, therefore, in the wicked world, no such fraternal relations can be looked for. Selfishness is the law of that realm, and our social philosophy must adjust itself to this law. This is what theology has taught us to expect in human society.

The political economy of the past has taken its cue from theology, and has drawn its deductions from the assumption that self interest is the ruling principle of human conduct.

Such have been the theories of social relations which have prevailed hitherto in Christendom. It must be confessed that our theories of society have been bad enough to produce a bad society;

and it must also be owned that they
have done it. There are plenty of people
yet who are ready to stand up for these
theories and defend them against all com-
ers. I am not here to take up that combat.
I am only here to say that whether they
are true or false, they are not the doctrine
of Jesus Christ. For there is not one word
that he ever said which, rightly interpreted,
could warrant the notion that God is
the Father of none but the good people.
What has he said in this very sermon?

"Ye have heard that it was said, Thou
shalt love thy neighbor and hate thine
enemy; but I say unto you, Love your
enemies and pray for them that persecute
you; *that ye may be sons of your Father
which is in heaven; for he maketh the sun
to rise on the evil and the good, and sendeth
his rain on the just and the unjust.*" How
can this doctrine of a partial Fatherhood
stand in the face of these words? Nay;

it is over all the children of men; even
your enemy is your brother, because he is
the child of your Father. It is not the
regenerate alone, but all who are made
in God's image, who come under the
law of brotherhood. All human relations
—domestic, economic, industrial, political
—are founded on this fact, and must conform to it.

Such is the teaching of Jesus Christ.
Such is the principle by which, in his
conception, society is to be constructed.

I have already said that many attempts have been made to build society
on other foundations. Indeed, it may be
said that all human society, up to the
present time, has been organized on other
than Christian principles; that as yet no
attempt has been made, on the large
scale, to realize a social order in accord-
ance with the principles of the Sermon on
the Mount. Most social philosophers have

stoutly maintained that the thing could not be done. Thus far in history human society has for the most part rested on an aristocratic basis. The fundamental assumption has been that some were born to rule and some to serve; or even that the many were created to be chattels and only a few to be persons. This social theory has been thoroughly tested, in its milder as well as in its harsher forms, and the verdict of the centuries seems to be strongly against it. It still survives, in great strength, in various parts of the world, but the foremost nations no longer avow it. There seems to be good reason for believing that it is gradually disappearing from the earth.

The existing social order in our own country, and among those peoples which seem to be most progressive, is somewhat ambiguous. So far as political institutions are concerned, they appear to rest upon the Christian foundation. Democracy distinctly implies the brotherhood of man. Its theory might perhaps somehow be worked out from a monadistic conception of the human being, and much of the earlier theorizing rested on some such conception; but fraternity has generally been emphasized by the champions of democratic rule, and we must suppose that the word has some meaning to them. Indeed, it will be found that democracy cannot be worked without a constant and practical recognition of the fact of human brotherhood. It implies not only a recognition of the equality of rights, but the purpose of all to protect the rights of each, and of each to respect the rights of all. The Golden Rule is the real foundation of every political democracy. The principle on which it rests is that each must do to others what he wishes that others should do to him. Patriotism in a democracy implies an un-

selfish devotion to the common welfare.
The patriot who is seeking office always
professes an altruistic regard for other
people's interests. He would not frankly
say that he wanted office for what he
could get out of it for himself, and that
he intended to make his constituents contribute to his aggrandizement. The appeal
that he makes assumes that the association
of men for political purposes is one in
which each should consider the welfare
of all the rest. Doubtless there is some
confusion of thought even here; for most
people believe that the office-seeker is not
entirely sincere, and the conception that
office is an opportunity of gain rather than
a post of service undoubtedly prevails.
Nevertheless, it is clear that political
democracy does connote a large conception of equality of rights and a habit of
coöperating for the common good. It cannot be maintained that the purpose for

which men are associated in a democracy
is a selfish purpose, or that individual
members of such a political society can
rightly govern themselves in this relation
by egoistic motives.

But when we come to those associations of men which are not political this
assumption of fraternal relations is at
once repudiated. Whatever may be the
bond that unites men, outside of their
relations to government, it is not, we are
often admonished, the Christian bond, the
bond of brotherhood. Men do not associate, we are told, on that basis.

What, then, is the basis on which they
do associate? Our society is not aristocratic; it is not feudalistic; it is not Christian. What shall we call it? "Industrial,"
they tell us. That is the word that de-
scribes it. Its basis is economic.

What does this mean? It means that
the main reason why men associate them-

selves in what is apparently misnamed
human society is not their interest in one
another, but their interest in the things
which they produce and possess and exchange. They form themselves into groups
because by this means they can get more
things and get them more easily. The
economic motive is the foundation of the
social order. Society is primarily useful
to a man so far as it enables him to increase
his stock of goods, including in this term,
of course, all that has exchangeable value.
It is admitted that men do unquestionably
derive other benefits from society than
those which are merely economic, but it is
asserted that economic benefits are the
fundamental reason for society. If this is
true, then the deepest relation of the social
order is not that of man to man, but of
man to things. And what is the nature of
that relation? It is not moral, of course,
for between a man and a thing there can

be no moral reciprocity. A man can owe
no duties to a thing, and a thing can have
no obligations to a man. The relation, as
Maurice says, between a man and the
earth, or the things of the earth, is dominion. He asserts his will over them; they
are his property. He does what he pleases
with them, and they are not able to call
his right in question. The great first thing
about a man in society, then, according to
this theory, is that he can exercise dominion. He realizes himself when he
asserts his will, when he brings his environment into subjection.

The assertion of this principle, or the
assumption of it, is bound to have consequences. If a man's first interest is in
things, it is inevitable that his relation to
things, which is that of dominion, will
become characteristic of him, will become
the dominant note of his life; and he will
naturally come to extend it, so far as he

can, over persons. The human relation, which is a moral relation will unconsciously be superseded by the non-moral relation to things, and we shall have, in what is called free society, the substance of slavery. The weaker will become, in effect, the thralls of the stronger. Make the basis of society economic, and you at once enthrone this principle of dominion, and slavery will be the outcome of it.

If you make property the basis of the family, that result will follow. "The language which is applied to one part of the family," says Maurice, "will gradually be applied to the whole of it. The belief in property will become the absorbing belief in the mind of the father; it will convert his authority over his son into mere dominion. It will be a question between the husband and the wife which shall have dominion over the other; notions of property will regulate the union.

Brothers will view their relation in the same aspect. It will be a struggle which shall possess most of that which the father leaves. Here is the test of the two principles. They will always be fighting in every man, to whatever society he belongs, democratical, aristocratical, monarchical. If he admits the principle of property in any case to be the ground of his connection with one of his own race, that principle becomes predominant in his whole life. If the domestic feeling is stronger in him than the feeling of possession, that will work itself out in him till it leavens his thoughts of everyone with whom he comes in contact."[1]

Thus the patriarchal idea, while it originally included slavery, finally destroyed it, for the human interest which recognized between master and slave was deeper and stronger than the property

[1] Social Morality, p. 78.

interest. The patriarchal system was primarily human and only secondarily economic. But modern slavery, which sprung from the slave trade, the slavery of the West Indies and America, was, as Maurice points out, the natural product of a society founded upon the economic motive. "The spirit of trade, the desire for property, must be credited with the origin of the traffic, with the maintenance of it, with the resistance to every proposal for abolishing or even mitigating it." The leaven of Christianity which is preserved in our political democracy has finally reacted against that grosser form of slavery and has abolished it; but the economic principle is still assumed to be fundamental in social relations, and it produces and must produce, so long as it is recognized as the constructive idea of our civilization, a state of things which differs from slavery only in name. The

better masters, in the old days of slavery,
were in the habit of pointing out to us that
our hired servants were often less kindly
regarded by us than were their slaves by
them. It was quite true. "It points,"
says Maurice, "to a tendency which is in
all of us—a tendency very little affected
by theories concerning government, not
touched by any of the contrivances or
comforts of modern civilization, strength-
ened rather than weakened by the mercantile dogmas which have supplanted the
old feudal dogmas. The habit of regarding
separate possession as the basis of society, as the end which all society seeks
to secure, leads directly to the expression
which we hear so often: 'I have paid the
fellow for his services. What more can he
ask of me?' That is, in other words: 'Between me and him there is no relation; the
only bond between us is that which money
has created.' That is the feeling on the

master's side. And the servant's, of necessity, responds to it: 'I owe him nothing; he has had his work out of me. What more have I to do with him?'"[1]

This is the result to which a society whose basis is economic must inevitably come. Labor, in such a society, will become a commodity, to be bought in the cheapest market and sold in the dearest. "Under an industrial regime," says Mackenzie, "character hardly counts. Personal relations become evanescent. It is no longer a case of one human being acting in concert with others or in subordination to them, but a case simply of a contract entered into between property and labor. The machinery is the agent; the persons are the instruments. . . . The sense of personal obligation has become less, or at least it has become far more difficult, than formerly to see definitely in what

[1] Social Morality, p. 83.

directions such obligations hold. The employer tends to become little more than an exploiter of labor, and at last an exploiter of himself; while the workman, in like manner, is apt to lose all consciousness of loyalty either to his employer or to his trade, or ultimately even to his own nature. Each is in the hands of a blind fate, a power, not himself, which makes for production; and to the dictates of this Moloch the well-being of each has to be subordinated. As the Greeks were said, when enslaved by the Romans, to have conquered their own masters, so it might seem as if, in a kind of inverse way, mind in conquering matter had become enslaved by it." [1]

Such is the logical and natural outcome of our social system, which, by its own confession, is not aristocratic, nor feudalistic, nor Christian, but is simply industrial,

[1] Introduction to Social Philosophy, pp. 100, 101.

finding the reason for its existence in economic relations. That a society in which
such relations are recognized as central,
primary, constructive, must produce just
such fruit as this is evident enough. That
it has produced much other and better
fruit than this is due to the fact that this
has not been the sole principle. Christian
ideas and motives have been all the while
at work in society, and they have greatly
modified the action of the economic force.
The worth of persons has thus been asserted, and the encroachments of dominion
have been restrained. Indeed, it has all
the while been admitted that Christianity
had valuable work to do in tempering and
modifying the action of the ruling principle; its chief function has been supposed
to be that of a lubricant for social friction
or a lotion for social inflammation. As
furnishing the law of human association
and coöperation, the world has scarcely

as yet begun to consider it. It is only just now, in these last years, that men are beginning to wonder whether indeed Jesus has any word of wisdom for our workday world; whether it can be to the striving, clamoring crowds of the street and the mart that he is calling, "Come unto me, and I will give you rest." That is a question that is worth pondering. Is it true that the way of Jesus is the way of life and health and peace not only for those who are preparing for heaven, but for those who are engaged in doing the work of this world? Is it true that the law of Fatherhood, with its corollary of brotherhood, is the fundamental law of all human association? Is it true that the enthronement of that law in the thoughts of men as the regulative principle of all their conduct in the shop, the store, the factory, the bank, the railway office, is the primary condition of successful social reconstruction?

For my own part, I find no difficulty in answering this question. That the real reason of society is not the relation of man to things, but of man to man, I find to be true physiologically and psychologically. With things we must have dealings, but our manhood is realized through personal relations. Gain is good, but love is life.

Shall brotherhood be tributary to prop erty or property to brotherhood? This is the question which confronts this genera- tion, and it calls on every one of us for great searchings of heart. It involves in its settlement some tremendous changes in our social life; it would overturn some of our institutions and abolish many of our customs, run its plowshare through our jurisprudence and give us some new reg- ulative maxims for the judgment of our laws.

To what extent these changes would affect our industrial organization I am not now prepared to say. Doubtless some industrial methods are more favorable and others less favorable to the promotion of brotherhood, and the worse should give place to the better. But it is far less a question of method than of spirit and purpose. I know some men who, with the machinery of the wage system, are realizing brotherhood as perfectly as I ever expect to see it realized in this world; and I know some who, with communistic machinery, have miserably failed to realize it. Where there are brothers there will be brotherhood—there and nowhere else.

That something can be done by better organization to give room and play to the spirit of brotherhood I do not doubt. We must make channels for the streams of love. But the fact is first; that will make its own form. And even before the fact must be the idea, the conception. That has hitherto been absent from the thoughts

of men, even of the followers of Christ.
They have not conceived of brotherhood
as the organic idea of human society, outside of the church. Until this conception
can enter and take possession of their
minds, there is not much use in organizing
social forms which wholly depend for their
efficiency on the presence and power of this
idea.

And I must express my serious doubt
whether this idea of the divine Fatherhood and the human brotherhood has been
grasped by many of those who are seeking
to reconstruct society along socialistic
lines. The philosophy which underlies
most of their schemes seems to me atom-
istic. The individual, after all, in these
theories, is the center of the universe. As
Mr. Bosanquet says, the basis of a great
deal of economic socialism is moral individualism. It seems to be imagined that
you can take a large number of egoistic

units, and, by adding them together in society in a certain way, get an altruistic result. I must be allowed to doubt it.

I have sometimes heard my socialist friends say that the social question is primarily and purely a question of bread and butter. That, as I have tried to show, is the fundamental assumption of the existing industrial order; and we have seen what kind of society it is sure to produce. Until we are able to see that our deepest relation in human society is not to things, but to persons—that man does not live by bread alone, nor even by bread and butter alone; that the spiritual facts outrank the economic facts—we shall make no very useful contributions to social reconstruction. And I beg my socialistic friends to beware how they proceed to tear down the existing order simply to rebuild it on the old materialistic foundations and with the same untempered mortar.

These criticisms are not intended to be sweeping and unqualified. Not all social-ists deserve them. Some among them per-ceive and emphasize the value of these deeper spiritual truths. And I hope that the day will come when we shall all be able to see that personality and not property is the primordial fact; that our relation to persons is deeper and diviner than our relation to things; and that there can be no enduring society which is not founded on the Fatherhood of God and the brother-hood of man.

I have devoted so much space to the exposition of the central idea of this sub-ject that I cannot dwell upon the applica-tions of it which the treatment itself sug-gests. How to realize this fact of brother-hood in the various social relations is a question to which we might well give more space than is now at our command.

How shall I treat my brother who is

associated with me in industry, my employee or my employer? It is hard to find a better answer than that of Mr. Mills: "Always do the loving thing." Let me consider his welfare as well as my own; let me take care that all my relations with him tend to his happiness, his welfare, his integrity.

How shall I treat my brother who is sinking into pauperism, who has come to possess the spirit of a mendicant, who is more than willing to live upon the labor of his fellows—nay, to take the goods for which they have labored and use them for his own destruction? Here is the explicit command of Jesus: "Give to him that asketh thee, and from him that would borrow of thee turn not thou away." Am I to obey this literally? Yes, whenever that is possible. "Give to him that asketh thee." He is your brother. Do not, if you can help it, turn him away. The

fact that he has appealed to you is proof
enough that he needs you. But be careful
what you give. It is not meant that you
are to give the specific thing asked for.
You may know that the thing wanted is
poison or some other means of self-destruc-
tion. You have no right to give that nor
the money that is likely to purchase that.
The big brother is not bound to give the
little brother open jackknives or hammers
and looking-glasses, even if the baby cry
for them. That is not a brotherly thing
to do. But he may give the love and care
which will satisfy the real need of the child.
Give to him that asketh thee. Give yourself, first. Give time and thought and
love. Give the kind of assistance that he
needs most. If he needs food give him
that, if you can without encouraging him
to be a mendicant. "We must learn,"
says Maurice, "what that precept means
by this sentence: 'Your Father in heaven

will not give to those who ask him for bread a stone, for fish a serpent.' He will not do men an injury merely to please them. If I regard a beggar as a fellow man, as a brother, I shall conform to the same rule. I shall not give him what would make him idle or brutal. I do turn away from him if to get rid of him or to please myself I degrade him." [1]

How shall I treat my brother who has become my enemy and tries to injure me? In the first place, I may probably assume that if all my own conduct has been right brotherly, if I have been seeking all the while to do good and not evil to all my fellow men, I am not likely to have many such enemies. But if there should be one who bears me malice and seeks my hurt, then let me remember Christ's words and patiently endure the wrong, returning good for evil. It may be questioned just how

[1] Social Morality, p. 391.

far this rule of nonresistance shall go. Most of these maxims are given in an absolute form, like the one on giving to him that asketh thee, and need to be interpreted with some judgment; nevertheless the spirit of this command is not to be questioned. It is far better to suffer wrong than to resist it. The quiet endurance of the injury disarms and subdues the enmity. There is power in this method of gentleness that the world knows not. Christ crucified is the power of God, mightier to subdue rebellion and violence than all the armies of the earth and all the hosts of heaven.

Such are some of the implications of the law of brotherhood. I fear that I have wearied you already, and I must not continue the study. We have only touched the surface of a theme whose meanings are deep and whose reach is wide. It has been my desire to get clearly before my own mind and your minds the real significance of Christ's teaching concerning the divine Fatherhood and the human brotherhood. If we accept these truths they must profoundly influence all our thoughts about human society.

Is the economic fact or the spiritual fact fundamental in human society? Are we competitors, or are we brothers? This is the central question.

Upon the answer to this question the peace and welfare of the nation, of the whole world, must largely depend.

II

Labor Wars

INTERNATIONAL wars are less common than once they were; their methods and implements have become so destructive that rulers shrink appalled from venturing upon them. It seems probable that the present war between Russia and Japan, by the frightful exhibition which it is making of the necessary consequences of strife between strong nations, will do more than has been done by any other event of history to make war impossible, and to hasten the day of universal arbitration.

For the wars of nations, however, we have substituted the wars of classes, which are waged in the industrial arena with other weapons than those of military warfare, but with great injury to all who take part in them.   I wish to consider with you this state of war which exists throughout the industrial world.   It is part of our business, as ministers of the gospel of peace, to put an end to wars of all sorts; and with this particular strife we shall have more to do than with any other.   We must, therefore, have some clear and definite knowledge concerning the nature of the conflict and the claims of the contending parties.   It will not do for us to take our opinions from either of them; we must be able to maintain a perfectly judicial attitude.   I greatly fear that the pulpit has not always succeeded in doing this.   Deplorable as the fact may be, the people in our churches, and those on whom we mainly depend for our support, are mostly on the employer's side in this warfare; the ranks of organized labor are not largely represented in our churches.   Our associations and our interests are liable.

therefore, to draw us into alliance with the employing class. We have great need to guard ourselves against this, and to keep our minds open to the plea of the wage-workers.

In taking up this question my own mind inevitably reverts to an experience of my own, to which I may venture to refer, as it illustrates what I have been saying.

In the spring and early summer of 1886 this industrial conflict was raging in various parts of this country in very acute form, and a man of good will in Cleveland conceived the idea of having a great meeting there, in which employers and employed should come together and be addressed by some one in the interests of peace. I had the great honor of being invited to make that address; and a large audience was assembled in the Music Hall of Cleveland, composed pretty largely of the workingmen, but containing also a fair representation of their employers. The subject of my address was the simple question, "Is it peace or war?" and I did my best to show those who listened to me that while the existing state of industrial society was a state of war, such war was both needless and wicked, and to point out to them how, by the exercise of justice and reasonableness and common sense and good will on both sides, it could be avoided.

I have been looking over that old address—made eighteen years ago—and I find nothing in it which I should care to alter. What interests me particularly, however, in my remembrance of it, is the way in which it was received by those who then heard it. For I repeated it, the next week, twice in Boston, once to an audience mainly composed of the employing class, once to an audience almost wholly made up of wage-workers; and the verdict of these three audiences upon my plea for peace was, to me, on the whole, very encouraging.

There were some employers, indeed, who put me down at once as a walking delegate—a representative of the unions, and who had no further use for me; and there were some workingmen who said that I was in the pay of the capitalists, like all the rest of the parsons, and who gave me a very cold shoulder. I think that every man who tries to make peace between these warring classes and who succeeds in holding the balances pretty nearly level—in being just to both sides—is perfectly sure to have that experience. There will always be those on both sides who, because he does not espouse their cause entirely, will deem him their enemy. That is the state of mind which war engenders. People who are at war never see both sides. For them there is but one side. Of discriminating judgment they are incapable, and those who are not fighting in their ranks they count their foes.

It was not true, however, of the majority of the audiences which listened to my plea for peace seventeen years ago, that they were in this unreasonable attitude; on the contrary, it was very cordially received by both sides. The sense of justice and fair play in which I know that it originated, and to which it made appeal, triumphed over the partisan temper, and *most* of these American men, of both classes, heartily applauded my earnest plea for a better understanding and a closer friendship between the men who organize the work and the men who do the work. That showed that although war then existed between the classes, there was, at that time, a general recognition of the fact that war is not a good thing; that the methods of peace are better than the methods of war.

I wonder whether this fact is as clearly recognized now as it was then. I fear that it is not. I fear that we have been drifting, ever since that day, more and more toward a condition of chronic warfare; that the relations between employers and employed are becoming, more and more, the relations of belligerents. And I think this a very serious and alarming state of affairs.

The main reason for this is in the fact that the years intervening between that date and this have covered the most gigantic movement in the way of industrial combination that the world has ever seen. In every line of industry and trade the number of independent establishments has been diminishing; the largest portion of the business of the country is now done by immense aggregations of capital, ranging from small combines which represent five or ten millions, up to the Steel Corporation with its capital of twelve hundred millions.

The effect of all this concentration of capital has been to widen the distance and deepen the alienation between the employer and the employed. The working classes generally regard those huge combinations of capital with grave suspicion. They fear that this power will be used for their oppression. It is a natural and justifiable fear. When capital becomes so massed and aggregated that it controls the larger part of any given industry, it is in a position to dictate terms to labor, unless labor also is combined on a scale equally extensive. It has the power to reduce or keep down wages; it can shut down its mills or factories in one place and supply the demand of the public from its mills or factories located elsewhere; the workmen of any one shop or factory are powerless to resist its oppression, if it is disposed to be oppressive.

One generally acknowledged purpose of

these combinations of capital has been the control of the labor market, the prevention of strikes by establishing a force strong enough to overpower the labor unions.

It is not, of course, wholly for purposes of war against labor that the great combinations of capital have been formed. There are other reasons. The elimination of destructive competition among the capitalists themselves is an important consideration; and there are certain great economies which may be effected through such combination. But it cannot be doubted that the purpose to which I have adverted, though not much advertised, has been constantly in view. It has been the dream of most of those who have been active in promoting the great consolidations of business that such tremendous forces would be adequate to deal with labor difficulties; that against their solid defenses the bat-

talions of the labor unions would dash
themselves to fragments. A great corporation which brings under one direction
some scores or hundreds of different concerns might, perhaps, hope to conquer in-
surrections of labor by fighting them in
detail, so that if the laborers in one of its
mills or furnaces struck for higher wages or
shorter hours, that mill could be promptly
closed and its business transferred to the
other mills or furnaces. That is not, indeed, a very farsighted policy, but we have
had abundant proof, of late, that men at
the head of great affairs are not always
farsighted; the narrowness and lack of
sagacity which they sometimes exhibit are
very conspicuous. But that some such
notion has had much to do with the rapid
centralization of industries can hardly be
doubted. Mr. Schwab, in his testimony
before the Industrial Commission, was non-
committal about the Steel Corporation's

policy on this matter; he was too shrewd
a man to proclaim any such purpose, or
even admit it; but it is probable that the
prodigious resources of these great companies have been relied on as giving them
a great advantage in labor disputes.

Dr. Albert Shaw, who is a keen and competent observer, and who has had abundant opportunities for watching the currents of public sentiment, said, some time
ago, that "Wall Street very much dreads
and dislikes what it calls a harsh and in-
discriminate attempt at the enforcement of
the antitrust laws, yet it has been indulg-
ing in the fantastic dream that with its
new and experimental weapon of industrial
combination it could at once go forth and
destroy so firmly established a force as
trade-unionism."

Whether this purpose has been consciously entertained or not makes, however, very little difference.   The consoli-

dations have been going on apace, during the past four or five years. The stars in their courses seem to have been driving the industries of the country into these great aggregations. If they have not been formed for purposes of war with the labor unions, they have been formed, and their existence is a new and formidable fact in the chronic dispute between capital and labor. They add immensely to the fighting strength of capital in the industrial conflict.

Of this fact the workingmen could not be ignorant. If a single laborer is practically helpless in bargaining with a corporation of the ordinary dimensions, and must take what he is offered or nothing, much less could he have any hope of getting his wishes or his needs considered in dealing with these colossal aggregations of capital. The individual sinks out of sight in such conditions. To say that every man must be free to make his own contracts with such a company is to misuse language; there is no freedom where there is no power, and the will of the individual employee is never for one instant considered by the great corporate employer. The terms are imposed on him; if he stands alone, he has nothing whatever to say about what they shall be. This is a fact which is often strangely overlooked by many of those who discuss this question. It is often assumed that the right and the entire right to fix the rate of wages, the length of hours, and the conditions of work rests with the employer; that when men venture to express their wishes they are usurping his functions, they are "trying to run his business." The examination of witnesses before the National Industrial Commission brought out ideas of this sort, now and then. One employer expressed the idea that it was all right for

workingmen to organize for the management of "their own affairs," but not for
the management of his. A little keen
questioning by one of the members of the
Commission drew from him some inter-
esting admissions:

"You said that you had no objection to
the workingmen organizing to manage their
own affairs. Do you not consider the
question of wages and the number of
hours that they shall work their own
affairs?"

"Yes, certainly."

"Do you not think that the thirty thousand men in your employ have as much
right to say what the wages and the hours
of work shall be in that trade as you
have?"

"Why, sure; we do not deny them that
right."

"You do not deny them that right?"

"No."

" Is not that practically all they organize for?"

"I do not know what they organize for. They have not bothered us about organizing. I have not heard anything about it."

"Would you consider it running your business, as you speak of, if they organized and wanted to consult with you, and confer with you, and fix hours and wages?"

"Well, *I do not know just how they would do it.* If they do as I have heard they have done, *I should not allow it. They want to dictate what we shall do.*"

The gentleman, as you see, is compelled to admit the abstract right of his thirty thousand employees to organize, providing their organization does not usurp his sacred and imperial prerogative of determining what their rate of wages and the hours of work shall be. That he will not allow. "They want to dictate," he says, "what

we shall do." That, of course, is out of
the question. It is rather for us, he means,
to dictate what they shall do.

This is the precise nature of the issue
which has been presented to the workingmen of this country by the formation of
the great trusts.

In the face of such combinations what
is the workingman to do? The force
which was formerly relied upon to equalize
conditions—the force of competition—has
practically disappeared; in its stead have
risen up these huge organizations of capital which have the power, and may have
the purpose, to decide every question in
which he is interested—the question of his
livelihood and his welfare—without con-
sulting him at all. Every single wage-
worker, under these conditions, is in a
condition of practical vassalage. What is
the workingman to do?

He may do one of two things. He may

accept the situation, complacently, in the confidence that the purpose of these great aggregations of capital is wholly benevolent, so far as he is concerned. That is what some of those on the other side of the line tell him he ought to do. That is what Mr. Baer said, so strongly, three years ago. "The rights and liberties of the laboring man will be protected and cared for," said this philanthropist, "not by the labor agitators, but by the Christian men to whom God in his infinite wisdom has given the control of the property interests of the country."

If, now, the laboring men feel entirely confident that this is true—that the property interests of this country, the trusts and the combines and the big corporations, have all been put into the hands of Christian men, genuine Christian men—if they are sure that the managers of all these great companies are purely disin-

terested and entirely philanthropic, and
that God has given them control of the
property interests of this country because
they are such men, and because he knows
that the interests of the laboring men are
perfectly safe in their hands—they may,
of course, very wisely dismiss from their
minds all concern about the future, and
accept with grateful hearts the bountiful
provision made by these agents of infinite
benevolence for their welfare and happiness.   And there are a great many employers (some of whom, I am bound to
admit, do not always appear to be so
philanthropic as they might be) who insist
that this is the attitude the workingman
ought to take; that a simple, childlike
trust of this nature in the benevolence of
his employer is the only becoming spirit
for him to cherish; and that when he
undertakes to arrange matters so that he
can have a voice in determining how the

product of his industry shall be distributed, he is making himself very obnoxious and detestable; he probably deserves to be called an anarchist.

But I think that most fair-minded employers must be able to see that this is a little more than can be fairly asked of the workingmen. Even Mr. Baer makes a large demand on our faith when he calls on us to believe that God has put into the hands of such as he is the welfare of the working people. That there are many conscientious and just employers we all know perfectly well; but that they are all such, or that those who are conscientious and just will be allowed to dictate the policy of the rest; especially that the great impersonal, soulless combinations of capital can be implicitly trusted to behave as if they were the vicegerents of the divine benevolence—all this is too large a proposition for the workingman to take on trust.

It is irrational for him as an intelligent man and a freeman to surrender to the arbitrament of these great powers all that most deeply concerns his physical well-being.

The only other thing for him to do is to invoke the power of organization for his protection. If capital organizes on the scale of a continent, labor must organize on the same scale. If capital proceeds to form combinations by means of which it would be able to crush unorganized labor, labor must proceed to form combinations strong enough to resist such aggression. There is nothing else for workingmen to do. If they failed to do it, they would not be fit for liberty.

The workingmen have clearly seen this, and they have met the emergency. Over against the portentous combinations of capital have risen up the equally portentous combinations of labor. Workmen of most trades are organized, and in their federations they have learned to act together with a considerable degree of unity. They sometimes fail to coöperate; the jealousies of leadership sometimes impair their coherency; but they are becoming more and more compact, and it may be expected that they will be able in the near future to present a solid front to the opposing host.

But is not this a tremendous power, you ask, which the wage-workers of the this country are thus seeking to wield? It is, I answer, a tremendous power. And is it not likely to be abused? Can such vast power be put into the hands of such men—for many of them are ignorant and narrow-minded and passionate—without great danger to the peace and welfare of the nation?

I answer that this power is, indeed, very likely to be abused; that it is certain to be abused; that it is already abused,

grievously abused in many flagrant ways—
just as the power of organized capital is
grievously abused in many flagrant ways;
in quite as many, I think.   It was evident,
beforehand, that we were confronting here
a great danger. It was evident that when
organized labor began to be conscious of
its power—after it had won one or two
signal victories—the tendency would be
very strong to push its claims to an extravagant excess; to be greedy and brutal
and tyrannical. The possession of great
power generally leads its possessors to be
arrogant and headstrong; it affects organized labor in that way just as it affects
organized capital. The great victory of
the miners three years ago led the unions
throughout the country to think they had
unlimited power, and that they could do
about what they pleased with it; and a temper was generated among them which boded
ill to the peace and welfare of the nation.

Instances of this soon began to appear.
One fact impressed me very painfully. I
know several employers who have always
striven to keep the relations between
themselves and their men on a basis of
justice and kindness—men who have stud-
ied the welfare of their men most carefully,
have given them always as large wages as
they could afford to give, and have tried
to do as they would be done by in all their
dealings with their employees. Between
these employers and their employees the
relations, until within the last two years,
have always been those of the most cordial friendship; they met on equal terms;
they consulted freely about their mutual
interests; no suspicions or fears divided
them. Somehow, these employers say,
these relations have been changed. The
men do not appear to wish to be in friendly
relations with them; they hold themselves
aloof; they repel overtures of familiarity;

they do not, apparently, wish to be seen in conversation with their employer; they appear to think him an enemy against whom they must be on their guard. I have heard large-minded and large-hearted employers speak of this tendency among their trusted employees with a deep sorrow. They could not bear to think that the old good will and affection between themselves and their men were waning, and they knew that they were not to blame for this state of things.

One or two sample instances illustrate the tendency which I am deploring, the tendency to reckless and irresponsible action on the part of the unions, which followed the anthracite strike. The case of Parks, in New York, who was convicted and sent to prison for blackmail—for extorting money from an employer as the price of stopping a strike, and putting the money in his own pocket—was not reassuring to those who have stood up for

the labor unions. There was no doubt
that this man was a scoundrel—indeed, he
was a self-confessed scoundrel—and yet his
union was determined to regard him as a
hero. That such a man could command so
large a following was discouraging to those
who see that the only salvation for the
unions is in the choice of wise and honorable leaders.

The facts which came to light in the case
of Martin at Washington were also dis-
quieting. It appeared that the union involved in this matter requires its members
to promise that they will regard their obligations to it as superior to all others—as
outranking those which they owe to the
state and nation. I do not know to what
extent oaths like these are imposed by
unions on their members, but I have no
hesitation in saying that they are in the
highest degree immoral and disloyal. Any
company of men which separates itself

from the commonwealth, and sets up
claims for itself which override the supreme
loyalty that a citizen owes to the nation, is
engaged in nefarious business. No such
organization has a right to exist under a
republican government. It is not possible
that the unions should hold their members
together on any such basis as this. The
workingmen of this country are loyal to
the nation; they will not suffer themselves
to be arrayed against the national authority. No demonstration made by organized capital against the liberties of the
country could be more alarming than such
an attempt on the part of the unions to set
their claims above the duty owed by their
members as citizens to the state or the
nation.

These are symptoms of a kind of in-
toxication which have appeared in various
quarters during the last three years. It is
quite as possible for labor organizations as

for organizations of capital to become "drunk with power," and to push their claims and demands beyond all the limits of reason and justice.

So, then, the thing which was to have been expected happened; the consciousness of great power acted on the labor union just as it acts on other people; it made them overbearing and unreasonable; it led them to make absurd exactions and impossible demands.

Well, then, some of you are asking, is it not a mistake to let them have this power? If labor organizations are liable to act in this way, why not forbid or discourage labor organizations? Why not organize to crush them?

This is the logic of the movement which has sprung up since the anthracite strike, and which aims to unite employers in a solid phalanx to fight the unions. The precise purpose of these employers' alliances it is not easy to state. Doubtless there are many fair-minded employers in their membership who merely wish to resist the unreasonable and unjust demands of the unions. An organization with such purposes is needed. Employers ought to stand together to protect themselves against unfair and ruinous exactions which unions sometimes seek to enforce. When there is firm organization on both sides, each will respect the other, and difficulties can be arbitrated with good hope of a just decision.

But there is abundant evidence that a great many of those who are pushing these employers' alliances are by no means content with such a just maintenance of their own rights. What they propose to do is to exterminate the unions. Sometimes this purpose is frankly avowed; generally, however, it is disclaimed; but the entire presentation of the case in the literature

of these associations shows that this is
their prevailing animus. The representation of the unions made in the various
manifestoes of these alliances is extremely
unfair and exaggerated; they are war
documents; they attribute only the worst
motives to the unionists and give them no
credit for justice or humanity. I have read
a great deal of labor literature which has
saddened me because of its unreason and
bitterness; but the literature put forth by
Mr. Parry's organizations, although ema-
nating from men whose intelligence ought
to have made them more temperate in their
statements, is about as discouraging as
anything that I have ever read. The evident intention is to create a hostile sentiment which shall result in their extinction.
The extravagance and injustice and rabid
partisanship of this movement came to a
head in the Citizens' Alliance of Colorado,
whose deeds of lawlessness and violence—

all done in the name of law and order—
certainly vie with the worst outrages that
have been committed in the cause of
unionism. Thus we find ourselves confronted with an organized, powerful, somewhat clamorous demand for the suppression of labor organizations. Those who
are engaged in this crusade often protest
that they are not opposed to labor organizations; but most of them when they are
narrowly questioned will say that so long
as labor organizations confine themselves
to their proper sphere and do not meddle
with the employer's business they are not
opposed to them, the constant assumption
being that whenever the unions venture to
say anything about the wages which their
members shall receive or the hours that
they shall work they are meddling with the
employer's business. The employer who
says that he is not opposed to labor organizations, but who objects to letting them

have any voice in determining wages or
hours of labor, is not quite ingenuous; for he
knows that this is the main purpose of labor
organizations.   It is like saying that you
have no objection to a church, provided it
doesn't meddle with religion, or to a government if it never has anything to do with
making or administering laws.   No; the
real fact is that we have now in existence a
powerful organization of employers whose
real purpose it is to destroy the labor
unions.   They would be willing that the
unions should live, if they would be content to be simply social or beneficial organizations, if they claimed no right to take a
hand in the settlement of the wages and
conditions of labor.   But they point to
the acts of unreason and injustice and lawlessness of which the unions have in so
many cases been guilty, and, in view of
these, demand their practical suppression.
Is this a reasonable demand?   That is a

question that some of you will be obliged
to face in the communities where you are
at work before many months. It is very
likely to be one of the burning questions of
your early ministry. What are you going
to say when men of your congregation,
your leading supporters, perhaps, tell you
of brutalities and vexatious and extravagant demands of the unions, and urge that
they are a nuisance and a curse, and ought
to be suppressed?

I think that it will be wise for you to tell
them that these acts of which they complain are undoubtedly very exasperating,
but that the remedy which they propose is
quite too drastic. It might be reasonable
to urge the extermination of labor organizations on account of their abuse of power,
provided you are prepared to apply the
same treatment to organizations of capital.
Shall we say that whenever any or some
corporations use their vast power lawlessly

or injuriously all corporations shall be
denounced or put under the ban of the
law? That will not, I dare say, be seriously
advocated.

Now, the fact is that the injury which
has been inflicted on society by the law-
less and predatory action of combinations
of capitalists is a hundredfold greater than
that which has been inflicted by combinations of laborers.   Yet most of us are able
to see that combinations of capital are
useful and necessary. None of us is so unreasonable as to dream of forbidding them.
We condemn the abuses, and we mean to
put an end to them, so far as we can; but
we shall still recognize and commend the
legitimate coöperation of capital in production.

We must treat labor organizations with
the same judicial fairness. When they
abuse their power let us condemn the
abuses, but let us clearly and strongly

affirm their rights. Workingmen have the right to combine, in labor organizations, for their own protection. It is simply part of the right of self-preservation. There is no other way, under the large system of industry, in which they can save themselves from social degradation and practical enslavement. No intelligent economist of to-day questions that proposition, and history abundantly confirms it. Many of the most intelligent employers of labor frankly acknowledge it. Yet this is the point about which to-day the battle rages. When this point is fully conceded by employers, when the right of workingmen to combine, and, through the principle of collective bargaining, to have a voice in regulating wages and hours of labor, is no longer questioned by employers, a great step will have been taken in the direction of industrial peace.

One thing is clear: The Christian minister and the Christian church ought to speak on this issue with no unwavering testimony. The rights of life and liberty are more sacred than the rights of property. The life and the liberty of the workingmen depend on their right to combine. That right all moral teachers must clearly affirm and maintain. To hesitate or quibble about it is to be faithless to our highest obligation. When we have plainly affirmed the right of the workingmen to live and to be free, and to make use of the only instrumentality by which they can secure life and freedom, then we may very properly reprove their abuses of the power in their hands. Until then our testimony against their outrages will have no weight with them, and ought to have none. The moral sense of the community will be effective in restraining the wrongs done by the unionist when the moral sense of the community unhesitatingly maintains his central and fundamental rights, and not until then.

The Christian church has occupied, quite generally, I fear, an equivocal position on this question, and for this reason the Christian church has lost its hold upon the working classes. It is a fatal mistake, and it cannot too soon be corrected.

May I show you now, in a few words, how I would treat this question by condensing what I said, not long ago, in a Sunday evening lecture, to both these contending parties? The first words are to employers:

1. The system of "collective bargaining" has come to stay, and it is well for you to learn to use it. It is true that it involves some disagreeable experiences. The trades unions are sometimes badly led, and they are sometimes arrogant and unreasonable, but the best way to cure these faults is to stand firmly on your rights,

but to treat them with perfect justice and perfect kindness. Many of the great employers have clearly come to this conclusion; the sooner the rest get round to it the better for them and for us all.

2. The rights of the nonunion man are sometimes supposed to be in the keeping of the employers. They argue that they must resist the union in order to protect the liberty of the nonunionist. But we have passed from the era of individual employers and of competition between individual laborers to the era of combinations; and collective bargaining is an essential feature of this system. If it is true that the liberty and the welfare of the workingmen in any trade can only be secured by union, then all the men of any trade ought to belong to the union. If I were a mechanic I should feel it my duty to join the union, and I might sometimes be convinced that it was my duty to stand with the union in

demanding certain improved conditions and in refusing to work unless they were granted. In such a case the man who stepped in and tried to prevent me and my fellows from securing this good would not be entitled to my gratitude, perhaps not to my respect. I should feel toward him, probably, something as our revolutionary fathers felt toward their neighbors called Tories, who refused to take part in the Revolution, and aided and abetted the British armies. Many of these were estimable men and women; they claimed the right to adhere to the government under which they had always lived; but we can hardly wonder that the colonists did not love them, nor that they made the country too hot to hold them. When men are struggling together and making great sacrifices to obtain a common good they are not likely to feel very amiable toward those who prevent them from gaining it.

It may be well for employers to try to get this point of view.

Now a friendly word or two to the workingmen.

1. You are claiming the right to exercise a great power. You must learn to use it wisely. You can generally win your rights by moderation and patience; you are pretty sure to lose if you resort to any other weapons. The great public on whose favor you must depend will always turn against you if you push your advantages in an unfair way. You won a great victory in the anthracite strike; you lost heavily, within a year, by making extravagant demands. You can easily destroy, by greedy exactions, the industries on which you thrive. That is not good policy, because it is unjust. You must learn to consider, in all these disputes, the rights and the interests of your employers, as well as your own.

2. Now about the man whom you call the scab. It isn't a pretty name, and I wouldn't use it; you will win, more surely, if you will learn, like John Mitchell, to be gentlemen. I don't ask you to like the nonunion man; I don't blame you for resenting his conduct; but keep your hands off him. Do him no harm. You have no need to resort to violence. It is always a sign of weakness.

" Thrice is he armed that hath his quarrel just."

That is the armor in which you must learn to trust. If your unions are as strong as they ought to be, as they will be if you are reasonable and wise, the non-union man will not count much in the struggle. You can win in spite of him.

3. You are sometimes accused of conduct that is of doubtful wisdom. You have sometimes resisted the introduction of improved machinery or improved processes; most of you are now too wise for

that, but it is well to be firm against such folly. You have sometimes sought to keep up wages by lessening the output; capitalists are silly enough to do this, now and then, but you must take a broader view. What cripples production must, in the long run, be an injury to everybody.

Your rules and restrictions sometimes have the effect to discourage talent and keep all workmen on a dead level; that is against the order of nature and cannot be maintained. There is no objection to a minimum wage, but there must be the largest liberty for those who have the power to rise. Any such attempts to enforce monotony, and prevent the growth of enterprise and genius, will assuredly bring stagnation and death to the organizations which adhere to them. Great Nature is stronger than you are, and she will have no such mechanical uniformities among her living children.

Finally, my friends, you who work for wages, and you who pay wages for work, the day has come when you must study the things that make for peace. You are both pretty strong for war, and, therefore, unless you are fools, you will both be able to see that war is out of the question. War never settles anything; the only way in which disputes among human beings can be rightly terminated is the way of reason and good will. Your disagreement with your neighbor is not rightly settled when you have overpowered him by force of arms and have made him submit to your arbitrament; it is never settled to your satisfaction, if you are a right-minded man, until it is settled to his satisfaction. That principle applies to all these labor disputes. The capitalist who wants to enjoy his combinations and their fruits, and at the same time wants to put down the labor union, has got something wrong in his head and in his heart of which he needs to get rid; the labor-unionist who expects to use his organization to subjugate capital and tyrannize over his fellow man is no whit better than any tyrant of the olden times. The idea that the ends of humanity and of civilization will be gained when one class— no matter which class—gets such a vast power into its hands that it can put down all other classes, is a very crude conception of the forces that make for progress— albeit it seems to lie at the basis of much of the wild talk that we hear on both sides of the labor conflict.

We are members one of another, and we must be helpers one of another—this is the basis on which men have got to learn to live together, and they will be scourged and punished by the reactions and devastations of their own selfishness, until they have learned this lesson. They ought to have learned it a great while ago. If they had not been full of moral stupidity they would have learned it.

War is the climax of unreason. It is the natural offspring of selfishness, and selfishness is the concentrated essence of foolishness. These wars of the classes are the stupidest and foolishest of all. It is just the right hand fighting with the left hand; they can bruise and maim each other; would it be a good thing if one could permanently disable the other?

It is all irrational and absurd, brother men, this warfare of social classes. You were not made to live together in this way. When will you stop your senseless fighting and learn to dwell together in peace and amity?

III

The Programme of Socialism

THE spread of Socialism is one of the phenomenal facts of the past decade. Ten years ago it seemed a mere dream; to-day it is not merely a hope, but a strong expectation in the minds of millions. You have read the reports of the German elections for the last three years; the Socialist Party in the Reichstag is now the strongest party; it is only by the combination of other parties against it that it can be held in check.

In our own country its political strength does not yet appear; but conversation among thoughtful men not only of the working classes but also of the educated classes will reveal the presence of large numbers who regard Socialism as the goal toward which society is moving. Doubtless the enormous growth of combinations, both of capital and of labor, has hastened the progress of opinion in this direction.

There are many who have been compelled to think of Socialism as the ultimate form of human society, who have never very clearly worked out in their own minds the programme of Socialism. Indeed, I think that the ideas of the Socialists themselves are often rather confused and indefinite. As to the practical programme there would be many differences of opinion among them. Many of the most intelligent Socialists of to-day do not propose any very revolutionary schemes. They would not change, radically and violently, the existing order. They would begin with certain reforms, and, when these had approved themselves to the public, would take further steps in the

same direction. Many of us, I think, would
go with them in the first stages of their
programme toward the socialization of industry, but we could not go all the way.
Therefore it is very important that we consider somewhat carefully not merely the
preliminary steps which they ask us to
take, but also the goal to which they would
conduct us. Then we shall have a fair
understanding not only with them, but
with ourselves.

The best elementary scientific statement
of the programme of Socialism that I know
of is Schaeffle's "Quintessence of Socialism." The aim of Socialism, Schaeffle tells
us, is "to replace the system of private capital by a system of collective capital; that
is, by a method of production which would
introduce unified organization of national
labor as a basis of collective ownership of
all the means of production by all the
members of the society. This collective

method of production would remove the
present competitive system by placing
under official administration such departments of production as can be managed collectively (socially or coöperatively)
as well as the distribution among all of the
common produce of all, according to the
amount and social utility of the productive
labor of each."

The nationalization or municipaliza-
tion of capital—that is the shortest phrase
in which the scheme of Socialism can be
expressed. The farms, the mines, the railways and steamships, the furnaces, the
factories, the machinery, the dwellings, the
goods in warehouses and in transit would
all be owned by the state or the commune.
There would be no more private business,
no more individual enterprise. Socialism,
says Schaeffle, "is opposed to the entire
arrangement of private credit, loan, hire,
or lease—not only to private *productive*

capital, but also to private *loan* capital.
State credit and private credit, interest-
bearing capital and loan capital, are in-
compatible with the socialistic state. Socialism will entirely put an end to national
debts, private debts, tenancy, leases, and
all stocks and shares negotiable on the
Bourse. At the most, it would only con-
cede compensation for such investments
by a payment in consumable commodities.
A permanent hereditary aristocracy of
wealth, whether landed or commercial,
founded on rent and interest, would be
impossible.''

It is not true, then, that Socialism opposes capital; it only opposes capitalists.
It provides for vast accumulations of capital, but it would make them the common
property of the whole people. All industry
would thus be under government control;
the civil service would include the whole
population, or at least all that were en-

gaged in the production and distribution of wealth.

Whether money as well as private capital would be abolished is not quite certain. Hertzka, in his fascinating "Freiland," contrives to retain it, and Professor Ely thinks that "the abolition of money is no necessary part of a conservative Socialism;" but Professor Graham assumes that it would be banished, and labor checks substituted for it; while Schaeffle asserts that "it is a matter of history that money was never used in any closed economic circle; it would, therefore, have to disappear in any close economic community, such as that of Socialism." How any kind of foreign trade could be carried on without a medium of exchange it is not easy to understand.

All consumable commodities would be produced, then, on government farms or in government mines or manufactories or fisheries, under the direction of government officials; the amount of production would be determined in each case by government statisticians and actuaries; the goods so produced would be transported by government conveyances to government warehouses, and would there be exchanged for labor checks, presented by those who had received them for services rendered in some department of state-managed industry.

The question of the distribution of the product of industry is answered variously and incoherently by the Socialist authorities. There is no consent among them; many of them refuse to offer any definite propositions. On what principle and in what proportion shall the various classes of workers share in the wealth produced? Schaeffle, in the definition quoted, assumes that the distribution will be proportioned "to the amount and social utility of the productive labor of each." But how to calculate this in such a manner as to satisfy all classes of workers is a problem to which no intelligible solution has yet been vouchsafed. In truth, the undertaking is quixotic. By what sort of alligation shall we determine how many days' work of a ditch-digger equal in social utility ten days' work of a watchmaker or an engine driver or a drawing teacher? These things must be adjusted, in the Social Democracy, by a majority vote; and it is easy to predict that there will be lively times in the Coöperative Commonwealth before the schedule of wages is finally agreed upon. It would be a more difficult question to settle than the tariff question or the currency question.

Mr. Bellamy cut the Gordian knot by proposing a communistic distribution— equal incomes to all, no matter what their social utility or inutility. But equality is not equity. "Nothing," as a German jurist has said, "can be more unequal than the equal treatment of unequals." Some men will make large contributions to this common fund by their industry, their intelligence, their efficiency, and their unselfishness; others—hosts of them—will be intentional malingerers and shirkers and spongers. To reward these classes equally would be a monstrous injustice. Nor can equality be predicated even of needs. Some need far more than others; one man will use productively and beneficently one hundred dollars a day; another man will get far more harm than good for himself and for the community out of one dollar a day. Are the needs of these men equal? "If we take men as they are now, or as they are likely to be for a long time," says Professor Ely, "we have every reason to believe that an assignment of nearly equal income would not enlist in socialistic pro-

duction the most capable members of the
community in such a manner that they
would give their best energies to the socialistic state; but unless we could secure from
the most talented members of the community willing service, Socialism would
inevitably prove a serious failure. The
poor organization and management of
the productive forces of society would lead
to far greater waste than that which we
experience at the present time. It is much
to be feared that men cannot be socialized
to that extent that they will generally
accept the principle of equal reward for
their services, even could it be shown
that it were desirable. And it is impossible to show this, for quite the contrary
is true."

I fear that large masses of the community are not socialized sufficiently to make
them willing to work at all, if by any
means they could get rid of work. I

speak with some knowledge, for I have been dealing for more than forty years with a good many people of this class, and I am sure that the proportion of them in society is rapidly increasing. The unemployed are many, but a large percentage of these are not merely unemployed—they are unemployable. Add to these the great multitude whose main purpose in life is to get something for nothing; who by all manner of schemes, devices, and plots contrive to worm their living out of society without giving anything substantial or serviceable in return for it. This class includes not only the gamblers and the swindlers, but also the promoters of hosts of visionary or preposterous enterprises, and a great army of pseudo-philanthropists. The parasites of industry are legion. And while the existing economic conditions may have much to do in developing this class, the fundamental trouble with most of those who compose it is a chronic indisposition to confine themselves to regular and patient industry. The difficulty in the case is in character, and no new arrangement of economic conditions would remove it. The problem which Socialism would encounter in dealing with such persons is likely to be very serious.

"Everybody," says Professor Naquet, under the socialistic scheme "will be compelled to labor, with the exception of the invalids and the aged. Here, already, a pause is necessary. The invalids and the aged will be free from labor. Quite so, and as to the aged nothing need be said, age being always easy to determine; but how about the sick? All the idle, all the do-nothings call themselves invalids; and how will it be possible to ascertain whether really they are invalids or not? There will be seen reproduced, on a gigantic scale, what takes place actually in the army.

Physical infirmities, easily ascertained, do not give rise in the army, and could not give rise in Collectivist society, to any kind of difficulty. On the other hand, the affections so numerous and so manifold of the nervous system, more painful a hundredfold for those affected thereby than physical infirmities, but which do not show themselves and are not outwardly perceptible—how shall we be able to ascertain these, and check the statement of those who pretend to be afflicted? Shall we believe on their mere word those who will say that they are stricken with such infirmities? In this case, what a number of idlers living at the expense of others! The actual amount levied by capital is nothing in comparison with the idling consumption which will be produced to-morrow. Shall we systematically refuse to believe the parties interested? Then what a number of innocent victims! What a number

of sick and infirm to whom it will be said,
' Either work or die of hunger'!"

Private enterprise will be forbidden in
the socialistic state, but private property,
we are told, may continue to exist. One
of the first questions to solve will be the
question of compensation to the expropriated. There are those who would not
trouble themselves about this; they would
simply confiscate existing property for the
benefit of the commonwealth. But others
are more generous, and insist that some
compensation should be allowed to those
who are dispossessed. The railways, tele-
graph lines, steamboats, mines, farms, factories, furnaces, mills, warehouses, with the
vast stocks of goods prepared for consumption, must be taken possession of by the
state; and those who now own them would
be entitled, say some of the Socialists, to
receive some return for what they are compelled to surrender. But there is no money

—nothing but labor checks, which are simply orders upon the warehouses for consumable commodities; and the ex-capitalists could have no property from which they could legally derive an income. It is proposed that their compensation be put into the form of a terminable annuity, by which an amount equal to the interest on the capital expropriated should be allowed for a certain number of years, after which the ex-capitalists and their descendants must take their places in the ranks and work for their living like other people. Such a compensation would, in some cases, enable the expropriated to spend profusely; and, if the labor checks were good until used, vast accumulations of them might thus be made.

Let us suppose that our friend Mr. Carnegie were thus relieved of his burdens; let us imagine that in return for his estate of three hundred millions an annuity equivalent to three per cent upon that sum were guaranteed to him and his heirs for thirty years. Labor checks supposed to be equal in value to this interest of nine million dollars would then be handed over to him annually. It is evident that he would be able to get all the groceries and dry goods and millinery and drugs and medicines that he would need out of that annual income; and he might even build several libraries and a yacht or two, and own several automobiles, and employ a great many servants. There would be no stocks or bonds in which he could invest his income; and he could not engage in trade, nor could he loan his income legally; the law would forbid that. But the laws of many states have forbidden usury, and they have been practically inoperative; and I doubt whether it would be possible for the state to prevent the possessors of large hoards of currency—no matter what that currency

might be—from employing it lucratively.
The prohibition of interest could be avoided as easily as the prohibition of usury
has always been. The borrower, giving his
note for a thousand dollars, might receive
in return for it only nine hundred. In the
agricultural communities of Russia, where
property is in common and interest is forbidden, the thrifty continually get the
advantage of the unthrifty by this very
method of usurious interest. The "Eaters
of the Mir" these lenders are called.

It is evident, then, that if the principle
of compensation be admitted, we shall
start out upon our socialistic experiment
with a large class of persons who will be
well equipped for luxury, for hoarding, and
for the gainful use of their accumulations.
There will be no enterprise in which they
can invest their surplus, and they will
therefore be driven to hoarding and to
illicit usury. "There would be some dev-

otees of joy," says Professor Naquet,
"who would spend every day their wage
of yesterday, and some saving people, and
misers even, who would pile labor notes
upon labor notes. What could prevent
one of these spendthrifts from borrowing
of one of these misers, and who would be
able to forbid the miser from granting a
loan?" There is reason to fear that the
money grubbers would succeed in being as
hateful and oppressive in that society as
they are in this. "There would be private
buying and selling and speculating," says
Professor Graham, "because the speculative—which is closely connected with the
gambling—spirit is so strong in so many.
Money would be won and lost, and the
necessitous, the losers, in spite of all prohibition would offer high interest to whom-
soever would advance money in the hour
of need. It is even probable, so long as no
interest could be made legitimately by any

investment of money, that this gambling
and speculative spirit would be enormously
increased. . . . If, in short, people can get
no interest for savings, and are not allowed
to invest them productively, one or other
of two things, both bad morally and materially, will result: either extravagant
unproductive consumption of luxuries, or
speculation, whether of a wholly gambling
kind or such gambling as that on the turf,
where there is room for special knowledge
and skilled judgment which make some
chance of winning. . . . On the whole, we
may say that the well-intentioned but am-
bitious attempt of the Socialists to suppress
money, the investment list, and the Stock
Exchange, would lead to much greater
visible evils than exist at present."

Whether our neighbors, the Goulds, and
the Astors, and the Vanderbilts, and the
Rockefellers, and the Carnegies, and the
Morgans, would be able to travel abroad is

not so clear, yet I dare say that they would manage it. Though we had no foreign trade, an occasional ship from other shores would anchor, perhaps, in New York harbor; and visitors who wished to tarry for a while in this country would be obliged to provide themselves with our labor checks, for which they would exchange English sovereigns and French napoleons and German twenty-mark pieces. The demand for these on the part of Americans wishing to travel would be so great that foreigners would be able to make very advantageous exchanges; but Americans could thus provide themselves with the means of foreign travel. It is a little bewildering to think of adopting a financial system which would put this nation completely out of commercial relations with all other countries; but there have been financial policies which seemed to look toward some such result at this.

I will not dwell upon other features of the socialistic regime which are often pointed out as impracticable or oppressive, for I am not sure about some of them; but the questions that I have raised make it very doubtful whether the complete nationalization of capital and productive industry is a practicable scheme. My own opinion is that it would raise more difficulties than it would solve; that while we should get rid of one set of abuses, we should bring in another set no less grievous.

Indeed, I am very sure that neither individualism nor Socialism furnishes a safe principle for the organization of society; but that what we need is the coördination of the two principles; and that the problem of statesmanship, henceforth, is the maintenance, in full force, of both of them, and the preservation of an equilibrium between them.

I have said this more than once, and am

perfectly aware that I am publishing no novelty; but it seems to me a truth which needs to be said over and over, in many kinds of phrase, that people may get accustomed to it, and understand what is the rational programme of social progress.

I think that for the normal development of human character, and the stable and fruitful organization of human society, it is necessary to have private property firmly safeguarded and private enterprise strongly encouraged by the state. I doubt if the individuality which is the essential good of human existence can be secured under any other regime. What we must have is a society composed of men who are men— not fragments of manhood, not cogs in a wheel, not parts of a machine, but independent, clear-thinking, self-reliant men, who can stand on their own feet and speak their own minds, and make each his own contribution to the sum of human welfare.

For the production of such men I believe
that private property is necessary, and
private enterprise also. The man must
have his own footing in the material realm.
In handling property, in using it, in saving
it, spending it, producing it, a man gets a
very large part of his intellectual and moral
discipline. He gets much injury, of course,
when he misuses it, just as he does when
he misuses any other kind of power, but
his manhood depends on knowing how to
use every kind of power.

I do not suppose that a man could de-
velop a true manhood unless he had a
body of his own, in which his proprietary
rights were absolute. There are living
creatures who have no separate bodies,
like the coral, but they are of a very low
type. Some of the cœlenterates are
thoroughgoing communists; for their bodies are inseparable and continuous—common property. But it is necessary to his

manhood that a man should have a distinct physical organism, which shall be absolutely his own. I think it is also necessary that he should have property rights in those things by which his body is nourished and sustained in life, and a large measure of freedom in possessing and using these things.

I have read many arguments to prove that individuality could be properly conserved and developed under a regime of common property—a regime in which individual enterprise was practically forbidden—but they have not convinced me. I am as sure as I can be of anything which has not been fully demonstrated by experience that the extinction of private enterprise—the complete nationalization of all forms of industry—would result in a distinct reduction in the intellectual and moral force of the people.

Yet I am equally sure that there are

many industries that can best be carried on coöperatively; in which all the people should unite to furnish the capital and direct the work. Several industries of this kind are even now in beneficent operation; the business of carrying the mails and the business of public education being chief among them. We shall extend much farther this line of industries, in which the whole people coöperate through their governments —municipal, state, or national. The railways, the telegraphs, the mines will at no distant day be owned and controlled by the people through their governments; and the public service industries of the city, which are practical monopolies, will all come under this law. Any business which is actually or virtually a monopoly must ultimately be owned and managed by the government. This means a large extension of industries managed on a socialistic basis. Such an extension is perfectly sure to come at no distant day. I think that the majority of the American people are ready for it now.

It is evident, therefore, that we have already gone far in the direction of Socialism, and that we are destined to go farther. Yet I do not think that we are likely to go all the way. I think that we shall coöperate through the government of the state or the city in many of our industries, with great advantage to ourselves; but that we shall leave, also, a great many important industries to be managed by private persons, under the system of individual initiative. Just as the post office clerks and carriers, and the customhouse people, and the school-teachers, and the librarians in the public libraries, and the people in the waterworks and in the municipal lighting plants are working for the government now, so a much larger number will be working for the government by and by in the industries which will be nationalized or municipalized; but there will also be a great many of us who will be conducting private industries, providing our own capital and managing them according to our own ideas.

If you ask where the logical stopping place is between private and public management I answer that there may not be any logical stopping place, but that logic has very little to do with the development of life; life is all the while flying in the face of logic, and it is very likely to do so in this case. If Nature wants a certain result she generally gets it without much reference to scientific exactitude. The trees are not constructed geometrically, and the rivers do not follow the line which an engineer would lay down for them. You can prove that if the railways and the telegraphs and the public service companies are taken over by the government

a great many other things must be, and
that, in the end, all industries will be collectively administered; but the facts will
confute your arguments. A great many
industries will remain on the old basis. I
do not think that agriculture will ever be
collectively conducted; and agriculture is
now and always will be the most important
of all the industries.

Art work of all sorts will refuse to be
brought under the socialistic regimen; the
artist, above all men, must have a free
hand. I venture this prediction in full
view of the socialistic predilections of Morris
and other artists. And I think it probable
that a goodly number of industries smaller
and larger will furnish room for the development of private enterprise.

What I expect to see—rather what I
should expect to see if I had another
quarter of a century to live—would be the
progressive coördination of these two meth-

ods of public and private enterprise: collective industry existing side by side with private industries, and no hard and fast line dividing them; the problem of statesmanship being all the while to maintain them both and reconcile them, so that neither shall override the other. I should expect to see this partly because my theoretical estimates of what is essential in human character and human society lead my thought in this direction, and partly because I see that this is the way that things are actually going.

In Germany and in Belgium, where Socialism has had a much more complete development than elsewhere, the tendency is strong among the Socialists themselves to modify their extreme views, and to admit the possibility of some reconciliation of the two principles of public and private enterprise. The last chapters of Mr. Brooks's book, " The Social Unrest," give us some remarkable facts illustrating the change of attitude on the part of these modern Continental Socialists. I am sure that as the progress of the years is bringing many individualists to see that some of our industries must be carried on coöperatively by the state or the city, so it will also bring open-minded Socialists to see that some of them cannot be, and that we shall thus gradually come to common ground.

Such peaceful evolution is the thing to be desired. Rash and violent changes in the industrial order are the things to be deprecated and dreaded. The greatest danger now in sight is that which arises out of the stubborn and desperate attempts, made by large classes of employers, to prevent the organization of labor. If the general public should join with such movements as those of which Mr. Parry is the leader, and should succeed in suppressing trade-unionism, or, at least, in discouraging the unionists so that they should feel that there was no chance for them to improve their conditions by present forms of labor organization, then you would see a rapid growth of Socialism. The very large increase in the socialistic vote in the recent elections was due to this cause. Wherever the attempts to stamp out trade-unionism have been most successful, Socialism has increased most rapidly; wherever the claims of unionism have been most cordially recognized, Socialism has made little headway. Every trades assembly in the country to-day is the arena of hot disputes on this matter. The socialistic element in these assemblies is arguing that the unions are powerless; that they cannot protect the laborer; that his only resource is the ballot; that the thing for him to do is to take the government into his own hands and reorganize industrial

society on a socialistic basis. Every
Socialist newspaper is taunting the unionists with their failures, and telling them
that they are fools to think that by their
methods they can keep themselves from
being oppressed and enslaved. If the
workingmen can be made to believe that
unionism is indeed a weak device they will
go over in troops to the camp of the Socialists, and we shall be in danger of having
our industries plunged bodily into the
vortex of Collectivism. Those who think
that there is no danger from this source are
quite unaware of the forces with which
they are dealing.

These are vast questions with which we
have to deal, fellow men, and we have got
to use in solving them a great deal of patience and common sense and sweet reasonableness. We have got a great deal to
learn, all of us, and we must keep our minds
open to let experience teach us.

If we could all get rid of our sectarianism
—the notion that our sect or our party is all
right, and that those who think otherwise
are all wrong, and not only wrong but our
natural enemies, with whom we are to
take no counsel, and whom we are to do our
best to exterminate and drive from the face
of the earth—if we could get rid of this kind
of intolerance, we should be able very soon
to come to some reasonable agreement
about these great matters. It is not so
very long ago that between sects in the
Christian church some such hostility existed; it exists still in some portions of our
country. The principal of one of the
American Missionary Association schools
among the mountain whites of Kentucky
told at a recent meeting of a father who
came to his school, a few days before, and
said to him, "Do you let Baptists come to
this school?" "Why, yes," said the principal; "we ask no questions about the

pupil's religious belief." "Well, you are wrong," said the father, vehemently; "you ought not to let any Baptist come to your school. I won't have my boy in a school where there are Baptists." And he paid the bill of his son's tuition and took him away. Something like that used to be common among Christian sects, but we have pretty nearly outgrown it. We have learned to feel that those who do not think just as we do about doctrine and ritual may yet be very good people, with whom we may profitably consult and coöperate.

This sectarianism among social reformers is, however, still in a somewhat acute stage. There are a good many individualists who think that Socialists are a kind of vermin, or a species of noxious beasts. A book has lately been written by a minister, which I haven't read, but whose purpose is, I understand, to prove this proposition. And there are still many Socialists who have an idea that those who are not Socialists are, *ipso facto*, not much better than thieves and robbers.

This was the almost universal feeling of Socialists twenty years ago. Their proclamation then was that the triumph of their cause could come only through violence. Liebknecht wrote in 1874: "Those who wish a new society must work directly for the destruction of the old one." "It is solely a question of force," he said, "which is not to be fought out politically, but on the battle field." The man who thought that the question could be peaceably settled was a fool.

The one thing which to the Socialists of twenty-five years ago was most obnoxious was religion and the church. "It is our duty as Socialists," cried Liebknecht, "to root out the faith in God with all our zeal; nor is anyone worthy the name who does not consecrate himself to the spread of atheism." Engel said, "We are simply done with God" ("Mit Gott sind wir einfach fertig"); and Scholl was cheered when he said, "We open war upon God, because he is the greatest evil in the world."

These early Socialists would not unite with any who did not accept their entire programme; they denounced as traitors and poltroons all who suggested any such alliances.

All this has vastly changed. There are ignorant Socialists in America who still reëcho those old cries, but they are behind the age—far behind the leaders of their own party. These men of broader wisdom over the sea wish it clearly understood that they have no quarrel with religion; some among them are writing to prove that "religion is an abiding fact in the life of the race." And they are not now refusing in Germany to consult and work with other people; they are ready to be friends with their neighbors whose theories differ from theirs, and to take half a loaf any time rather than go hungry. Nor do they wish to gain their end by violence.

In short, it is true of the Socialists of Germany and Belgium that they are far less bitter and violent than once they were; that they have abandoned many of their extreme notions, and are ready, with their faces toward the goal of nationalized industry, to make haste slowly.

So, then, we may hope that the intolerance of the social sectarians will yield to the broadening light, as that of the religious sectarians has done, and that we shall be able, by and by, to reason together, and to find ways of organizing our industries which shall conserve individuality and strengthen the bonds of brotherhood.

IV

The True Socialism

My theme assumes that there is a true Socialism; that in the various discordant and incoherent movement of opinions and feelings and activities which goes by the name of Socialism there are mingled wholesome sentiments and reasonable aims.

We are safe in making this assumption. The spread of beliefs which are more or less correctly described as socialistic has been very rapid, both on this side of the ocean and on the other, during the last twenty-five years. Not merely the workingmen, but the students, the thinkers, have been profoundly affected by it; a great multitude—some of them blindly, noisily, passionately; some of them with their eyes open and their mouths shut—are traveling in the direction pointed out by the socialistic theories. It is perfectly certain that such a movement cannot be wholly the product of unreason and stupidity. It is not wise to denounce Socialism and Socialists hotly and by wholesale, as so many do; it is much better to try to understand what they have to say and to discern the truth which is mingled with what we may admit to be their errors and exaggerations.

When I speak of Socialism and Socialists no intelligent person will understand me as referring to Anarchism and Anarchists. The two are often confounded; and in the mêlée of the streets ignorant devotees from either side run together and lift up the same cries. But logically they are as far apart as the east and the west. Their only agreement is in dislike of the existing social order; when they begin to talk of what shall take its place they are antipodes. The Anarchist denounces gov-

ernment as essentially evil; he proposes to
abolish governmental restraint and direction; he insists that every man be
allowed to do that which is right in his own
eyes. Such associations for domestic or
industrial purposes as men choose to make
—such as spring up spontaneously after
the existing order is destroyed—are the
only forms of social order that he will tol-
erate. Doubtless men will group themselves in communities, even if there be no
political organization; and these communities will be loosely associated for
various purposes; but the Anarchist rejects
with scorn all existing social and political
institutions; in his scheme the only co-
hesive force is the natural social instinct.

The Socialist, for his part, proposes to
extend the powers of the state in every
direction. Government, with him, instead
of being an evil and a curse, is the medium
and minister of all social good, the custo-

dian that guards men's rights, the providence that guides their steps and secures their welfare. The Socialist proposes to enlarge the sphere of government until it covers almost the whole of human life.

Such is the fundamental antagonism between these two systems. The Anarchists are, philosophically, much more closely allied to the old school of political economists than they are to the Socialists. Anarchism is *laissez faire* reduced to its lowest terms. Herbert Spencer is the great philosopher of the Anarchists; they publish and circulate his books, and fortify their arguments with his reasonings. If I quote a few sentences of his you will see that this is good policy for them.

"As civilization advances," says Mr. Spencer, "does government decay. To the bad it is essential; to the good, not. It is the check which national wickedness makes to itself and exists only to the same degree.

Its continuance is proof of still existing bar-
barism." [1] "Government is an institution
originating in man's imperfection; an institution confessedly begotten by necessity
out of evil; one which might be dispensed
with were the world peopled with the
unselfish, the conscientious, the philanthropic; one, in short, inconsistent with
the highest conceivable perfection." [2]

"Nay, indeed, have we not seen that
government is essentially immoral? Is it
not the offspring of evil, bearing about it all
the marks of its parentage? Does it not
exist because crime exists? . . . And must
not government cease when crime ceases,
for the very lack of objects on which to
perform its function? Not only does mag-
isterial power exist *because* of evil, it exists
by evil. Violence is employed to maintain
it, and violence involves criminality. Sol-
diers, policemen, and gaolers, swords, bat-

[1] Social Statics, p. 25.   [2] Ibid., p. 25.

ons, and fetters are instruments for producing pain; and all infliction of pain is in the abstract wrong. The state employs evil weapons to subjugate evil, and is alike contaminated by the objects with which it deals and the means with which it works." [1]

This is the precise philosophy of Anarchism; Mr. Justus Schwab could not be so explicit, and Mrs. Lucy Parsons could not more strongly express herself in any words of her own.

Socialism is the exact opposite of this doctrine. Karl Marx, Maurice Hyndman, William Morris, Edward Bellamy insist that as civilization advances government grows; that it is the institution by means of which man reaches perfection; that, instead of being the offspring of evil, it is the vicegerent of God.

I do not propose to take sides with either

[1] Ibid., p. 230.

of these antagonists, or to help them in fighting out their battles. The proper function of government is not now my theme. Doubtless, if I were forced to the confession of my own faith, I should be found standing a little nearer to Karl Marx and the Socialists than to Herbert Spencer and the Anarchists. But the distance between them is so vast that one may be very far from one without being very near the other.

Nevertheless, many of us who are not ready to own ourselves Socialists feel very strongly the evils of which they complain, and we are ready to go as far as we safely may in the direction in which they would lead us. The inequality of conditions, steadily increasing — pauperism growing as wealth grows; men by the million standing idle in the market places, for years at a time, while granaries are bursting and warehouses are groaning with the goods for lack of which the idle toilers are starving—these are features of the existing industrial regime that cause us no little solicitude. But these are not the worst symptoms of the disorder under which we are suffering. The increasing alienation and enmity by which social classes are set against each other; the spite of hand-workers against brain-workers; the cold, hard, haughty temper of the House of Have and the envy and hatred of the House of Want—these are the signs of the times that are most ominous. We may not, all of us, like the outlook in the direction of Socialism; but we are by no means content with the unsocial tempers and tendencies that find constant expression among us.

After all—and this is the thought that will detain us for a little while—it is the tempers and the tendencies of social life that are of most consequence. Where these are right the methods and the institutions will quickly adjust themselves to the needs of men. Roscher somewhere says that the communistic scheme would work beautifully among people who were fully possessed by the Christian spirit and purpose. But, then, he goes on, the wage system would work beautifully, too, in the hands of such people. It is just as true of sociology as of religion, that the letter killeth but the spirit giveth life. That some improvements can be made and must be made in the form of industrial and social organization I do believe; that these improvements will take the general direction of what is known as scientific Socialism I have no doubt; nevertheless the deepest need is not a change of forms, but a change of aims and purposes and tempers. What Paul said about Judaism may be said with equal force about Socialism: He is not the best Social-

ist who is one outwardly, who puts his
trust in statutes; neither is that the true
Socialism which is outward in the flesh,
which deals wholly with the machinery of
production and distribution; but he is a
true Socialist who is one inwardly, and the
genuine Socialism is that of the heart, in
the spirit, not in the letter.

And what is the spirit of the true Socialism? It is manifest, as I think, *in the
habit of regarding our work, whatever it may
be, as a social function.* The true Socialist is one who never forgets that he is a
member of society, and who always considers well the effect of what he is doing,
not merely upon his own private fortunes,
but also upon the common weal.

Do I seem to be giving utterance to a
commonplace? Bear with me, for a little,
and you will see that it is by no means so
much of a truism as it ought to be. Indeed,
I am venturing, somewhat rashly, no

doubt, to contradict many of the greatest authorities in social science who have written during the last century. The notion that a man should regard *his work* as a social function is not a familiar notion. The universal assumption is that the calling which a man follows is a means of livelihood or of personal aggrandizement; the question how the society in which he lives will be affected by it is one that scarcely suggests itself to the average man.

The minister of the gospel is, indeed, by many persons believed and expected to choose his calling with considerable reference to the good that he can do; yet he is by most people supposed to be mainly occupied with getting people safely out of this world into another rather than in improving the conditions of life in this world. And those who consider that his calling has something to do with making a better

world of this generally speak of his work
as if it were in this respect wholly excep-
tional—as if doing good were a business
of which he had the practical monopoly.
Possibly some persons would rank the
function of the teacher also in part, at
least, as a social function; they would say
that the teacher, by his profession, is a
servant or helper of the community. Of
the physician, most of us would hardly
admit so much. His office may be to
relieve individual suffering; but his connection with the social well-being is not
emphasized.

And when you come to those who are
employed in the great industries of production and distribution and exchange—
the farmer, the miner, the merchant, the
manufacturer, the banker, the mechanic,
the day-laborer—who thinks of these callings as being social functions? Who sets
before him as his distinct thought in

choosing a calling of this nature, and in pursuing it, "This work I will do that I may help to make the community in which I live happier and worthier"? Can such persons be found? Certainly they can. Here and there is one who does consciously and honestly connect his work with the common weal and set his will to the task of serving society, but that is not the habit of the multitude. The man who should profess that this was his purpose would be pretty sure to be regarded by the majority as a crank or a hypocrite. One's calling, one's lifework—that is primarily, chiefly, almost exclusively a means of livelihood or a means of advancing one's personal interests. One must, of course, be more or less public-spirited outside of his business; but his business itself is a purely individual affair.

Indeed, this is the doctrine, as I have said, of the political economy which was

taught in England and in America for a
hundred years. The fundamental assumption of that system was that a man will
seek his individual interest without regard
to social welfare; and its contention was
that he ought to do so, that when he made
self-interest his sole motive, and pushed
steadily in the direction in which that
would lead him, he was working in the most
effectual way for the public welfare. It
is futile and preposterous—so these teachers have said—for a man to mix any social
aims with his breadwinning or his fortune-
building; let him look out for his own interests, and leave the promotion of the
social welfare to the working of the natural
economic harmonies. "Every man and
woman in society," says one who repre-
sents this social philosophy, "has one big
duty: that is to take care of his or her
own self. This is a social duty. For, for-
tunately, the matter stands so that the

duty of making the best of oneself individually is not a separate thing from the duty of filling one's place in society, but the two are one, and the latter is accomplished when the former is done."

There! that sets before you, with clearness and precision, the substance of the Unsocialism which I am trying to describe to you. Let us think about it for a little while.

"One big duty," says this teacher, rests on "every man and woman" in society. And this big duty swallows up every other obligation, as Aaron's rod swallowed up all the other rods of the magicians. It is not, as in the ethics of the Christ, one great commandment, "Thou shalt love the Lord with all thy heart," and another like unto it or equal to it, "Thou shalt love thy neighbor as thyself;" it is one great commandment, one big duty, that dwarfs all the rest: Thou shalt love thyself supremely.

"This is a social duty," our philosopher assures us. "For taking care of one's own self is not a separate thing from filling one's place in society, but the two are one, and the latter is accomplished when the former is done." Wendell Phillips used to tell of a discontented wife who said that she had always heard that the man and his wife were one, and she had found out that it was true, but the man was the one. Our professor in like manner insists that self-interest and public spirit are one, and that self-interest is the one. His egoistic lion and his altruistic lamb lie down together— the lamb inside. The one big duty is to take care of yourself—to mind your own business.

Notice that this statement sweeps the field. "Every man and woman in society has one big duty: that is to take care of his or her own self." Well, to begin with, there are a good many thousands of men and women in society who occupy positions of public trust in the public service. This universal rule includes them. The people in all the offices, national, state, municipal—our judges, congressmen, executive officers, legislators, civil servants, along with the officers and men in the army and the navy—shall we say of these, of one and all, that every man and woman of them has one big duty: that is to take care of himself? Is that the supreme duty of every public official—to look out for himself, to feather his own nest, to make hay while the sun shines? Such, I am well aware, is the practice of a good many of them; but it is not their commonly avowed theory. It is true that the habit of regarding the public offices as spoils, to be distributed among the friends of successful candidates, is based on this theory, and cannot be justified for a moment on any other. Every advocate of the spoils sys-

tem believes in his heart, whatever he may
say with his lips, that office is mainly a
perquisite; that the main business of the
man who holds it is to look out for himself.
Beyond a question it is this view of public
office which has debauched our politics. Yet
I suppose that very few, outside the ranks
of the professional politicians, would deny
that this is a false and mischievous view.
Surely it is not the one big duty of the man
who holds a public office to take care of
himself. Let us grant that he may consider his own interests; that he may wish
and work for promotion; that he may
give due weight, in his efforts to secure the
office, to questions of salary and of honorable position; that he may allow personal
considerations of this nature a great deal
of influence over his judgment; let it be
granted that the average citizen is not
likely to serve the state from motives
purely and exclusively disinterested; still

it will remain true that the man who holds
a public office has something else to think
of besides taking care of himself. His one
big duty, whatever else it may include,
must involve the obligation to look out
for the interests of the community which
has intrusted him with this office. He is
there not merely or mainly to draw his
salary, and look after the primaries, and
keep the wheels of the party machine
properly oiled with a view to his own re-
ëlection or promotion; he is there that he
may work for the public welfare; that
he may protect society against injury or
minister to its needs. Surely this man
must have social instincts, social aims, a
sympathetic conscience that identifies his
welfare with the public welfare, a habit of
taking thought for others and not for himself alone. Multiply this man by several
hundreds of thousands, and you have the
numerical description of a pretty large

class of persons to whom, very obviously, this maxim cannot be applied.

Now the question arises whether the principles of morality change when a man passes from private station to public office. Is there one ethical law for the magistrate or the official and another for the citizen? Is the "big duty" of the one of a different nature, fundamentally, from the "big duty" of the other, calling forth different sentiments, inspired by different motives? Must the one consider, all the while, what the effect of his conduct will be on the welfare of society, while the other never gives this matter a thought? If this be so, if the morality of the man in office is different in kind from that of the man out of office, the case is certainly unfortunate; for men are constantly passing from the one condition to the other, and a man who has been trained in the unofficial methods of thought and judgment will not be at all prepared for the services of the state. The man who has always believed it his one big duty to take care of his own self and has learned to look with contempt on people who have any other aim in life, is very apt, if he gets into office, to go right on believing the same thing, and living up to it, too. It is difficult for him to divest himself of those habits of mind which have become part of his nature, and to begin to think and act with public interests continually in view.

But it is, of course, wholly absurd to talk about one standard of morals for people in office and another standard for people out of office. The fact that my neighbor is a member of the Common Council while I am only a private citizen does not make any radical difference in our obligations. Duty for him is essentially the same as duty for me. He ought to take care of himself and at the same time to study carefully the welfare of the society in which he lives, and so ought I. His official position may give him more opportunities to promote the welfare of society than mine gives me; but it is my duty to use with all good fidelity such opportunities as I have. The business of studying and promoting the general welfare does not devolve exclusively on the people who occupy the public offices.

I suppose that what I am saying now would be admitted by most of us. You will say again, "This is a commonplace; tell us something that we haven't heard so many times." Doubtless the notion that we must all take an interest in the public welfare is sufficiently familiar; we say it often enough; whether we do it to any great extent may be questionable. But our care for social welfare, be the same more or less, is generally disconnected from our private enterprise. While we are working at our trade, managing our business, following our profession, we consider that we are attending to what the professor calls our one big duty of taking care of our own selves; sometimes, in our leisure moments, we give thought and effort to the interests of the society in which we live—that is one of our little duties. Either through political instrumentalities or by means of social appliances of one sort or another we try to improve the community. We are not wholly destitute of public spirit; but public spirit is public spirit, and business is business. The two are wholly dissociated in our thought and our practice.

There is an important distinction to be made just here, which our professor can help us in making. The common notion is, he says, "that one has a duty to society as *a separate and special thing;* and that this duty consists in considering and deciding what other people ought to do." Now,

if there is any such common notion as that
I, for one, am not concerned to maintain
it. Minding other people's business is an
enterprise to which I have no inclination.
But it seems to me that the alternative of
exclusive selfishness is not necessarily meddling with other people's business. A man
may believe that his one big duty includes
something else besides taking care of his
own self without believing that it "consists in considering and deciding what
other people ought to do."

Three classes of men will come distinctly
into view if we carefully consider the
relations of individuals to society:

The first class—for it is better to get
rid of them at once—consists of those who
neglect their own business and devote
themselves to meddling with the affairs of
their neighbors, to "considering and deciding what other people ought to do."
These people are, no doubt, great nuisances.

Society has no use for them. It is quite proper to admonish them to mind their own business. It is no part of our duty to meddle with our neighbors' affairs, unless our neighbors are pursuing courses of conduct which are injurious to society. When they do that they must be restrained. But when we restrain them we are not really meddling with their affairs; we are attending to our own.

The second class consists of those who follow the counsel we are considering, and make it their one big duty to take care of their own selves, giving themselves no anxiety about what happens to the rest of mankind. They may feel that they have some relation to the society in which they live; but they have been taught, and they believe, that if they dismiss from their minds all care about the welfare of the community and devote themselves keenly and strenuously and exclusively to caring for their own selves, the welfare of the community will be secured; that an uncompromising and relentless individualism is the straight path to social peace and prosperity. They have been taught this, I say, and they believe it; but there is nothing more false, in Sheol or out of it, than this doctrine. It has been dinned into the ears of three generations, and it has been the maggot in the brain of the last century that has wrought the social madness which now disturbs our peace. You might as well expect that society would become reverential and devout by teaching every member of it to swear and blaspheme; or that it would become chaste and pure by making it the big duty of every man and woman to violate all the sanctities of sex, as to expect that it would become peaceful, harmonious, and prosperous by training everyone to care exclusively for his own self. The idea that social well-being is best promoted by the diligent employment of purely unsocial forces is an idea that the future will preserve, I think, among the curiosities of science.

The third of the classes to which I referred consists of those who make it their duty not merely to care for themselves, but also to consider the welfare of the community in which they live, and especially to see to it that the work by which they gain their livelihood tends to the improvement rather than the detriment of society. They think that the good citizen ought to be working for the good of the community not only in his leisure hours, but also and especially in his daily vocation; not only in the time that he devotes to politics and charity and religion, but also and much more effectively in the time that he devotes to business. And this not unconsciously, but purposely; not because he cannot help it, but because he counts it his high calling, an integral part of his big duty. They think that a man is bound, steadily and conscientiously, to consider the effect of the work he is doing not merely upon his own private fortunes, but also upon the society to which he belongs. They think, in other words, that every man ought to regard his calling, no matter what it may be—whether he is parson or plowman, whether he is surveyor or street sweeper, whether he is employer or wage-worker—not only as a means of personal advantage, but also as a social function.

He ought to regard his calling as a social function, because it is a social function. Every day this fact comes into clearer light. "The solidarity and interdependence of the modern economic world," says a late strong writer, "makes the old individualism an absurdity. From a modern economic point of view there is no such thing, in strictness, as a mere individual. Market prices, wages, profits—all these are social, not individual, products. Everyone's economic acts more or less affect everyone else; and everyone is dependent on others for the means of economic action." The market price of a loaf of bread, of a day's labor, is fixed not by the individual, but by the social organism. A thousand different forces combine to determine it. The social estimate of what your day's work is worth—that is what your day's work will bring you. Thus society continually acts upon you, shaping the issues of your life. And you, by your choices and efforts, are as constantly acting upon society. By what you do, by what you say, by what you are, society is affected in its economical, its ethical, its political interests. Most true is it—how much more true to-day than when the great apostle said it!—that no man liveth to himself.

The society in which you live, the customs, institutions, sentiments of the people among whom you live—these are your environment. And is it not a well-worn truth that life depends on the harmony between the organism and its environment? Can a man live healthily and happily in a bad environment? Must he not have good air to breathe, pure water to drink, safe shelter from the cold, nourishing food within reach? Is it of no consequence to a man what his environment is or how he is fitted to it? Could we wisely say to him, "It is your one big duty to go on living, no matter what the conditions of your life may be; to keep breathing, whether you have any air to breathe or not; to keep eating, let the food be wholesome or poisonous"? It is equally absurd to tell him to think only of his own interests and have no care for the society in which he lives. He cannot care for himself at all without keeping himself in the closest and most vital relations with the society in which he lives. And it makes a mighty difference to him, whether he knows it or not, what are the conditions of the society in which he lives.

We have found out that the physical environment can be improved by vigilance and care on the part of the community. We can exterminate some of the breeders of pestilence; we can purify the air and the water; we can abolish nuisances; we have actually extended, in this way, the average term of human life. Is it preposterous to suppose that the social environment may by patience and intelligence be somewhat improved? Might not the social atmosphere be made more wholesome and more vital? The sentiments, tempers, tendencies, customs of society, saying nothing of its institutions and its laws—might not they be rendered more genial? "Social laws," says Dr. Bascom, "are modifiable, and are suffering constant modification in the progress of society. This fact arises from their very nature. They rest on motives, incentives in the human mind, and these incentives are variable under social progress. Action and growth change the data from which the laws spring, and so change the laws themselves. These changes may be made successfully of set purpose as well as by insensible transformation."[1] The social environment, as well as the physical environment, can be improved without treading on any man's rights or meddling with any man's business, and the true Socialism teaches that it is part of every man's big duty to do what he can to improve it.

This discussion has, I trust, made it clear to most of us that our private enterprises ought to be inseparably linked with

[1]Words of Christ, p. 193.

social aims.   It justifies every man in laying down these propositions:

My business is not my business alone, and cannot be; it is a matter of vital concern to the society in which I live.

It ought to be managed, certainly, in such a way that society shall take no detriment from it; if possible in such a way that society shall be clearly benefited by it.

These principles, if we adopt them, may throw light upon the choice of a calling. That is a question of some consequence to some of the young men and women before me. "What shall we do?" they are asking. "To what calling shall we devote our lives?" It is a serious question, and it is only in a negative way that one man can answer it for another.   But if these reasonings are sound, then it is evident that no kind of work can be chosen the effect of which must be, in the long run, injurious to society.   Under the principle that it is every man's big duty to take care of his own self, almost any vocation can be chosen; but this higher principle rules out a good many callings that men find lucrative. Society, in its blindness, still rewards its foes about as liberally as its friends; enriches the men who are working to destroy it even more abundantly, in many cases, than the men who are trying to save it. But this fact does not justify the destroyers. A calling, like that of the liquor seller, may be lucrative, and may result in some incidental benefits; but if the net results be injury to society the True Socialism forbids and denounces it.

The calling of the gambler, of every grade of gambling, from the dealer in margins on 'change to the shooter of craps in the alley, falls under this condemnation. The gambler gets his living out of society without rendering any return therefor. He takes what he can get, and he gives nothing in exchange for it—no commodity, no service, no instruction, no accommodation, no innocent pleasure, nothing whatever. This is true of all who follow the gambler's vocation, whether in the boards of trade or in the dens of the bunko steerers. They are therefore social parasites; their economical status in the community is precisely the same as that of the sneak thieves and the beggars. It is a little queer that society still tolerates so much of this unsocial conduct. But it is evident that the gambler's calling will never be intelligently chosen by any man who is not willing to array himself with the enemies of society.

I will not stop to name the various callings which are excluded from your choice by this principle. It is more important to call your attention to the fact that the principle will determine not only what kind of work you will do, but the manner in which you will do it. For one can manage the humblest lawful business in such a way as to benefit society; and one can mismanage the most honorable business in such a way as to make it a curse to society. The scavenger "with this clause" is a public benefactor, and the lawyer who deems it his one big duty to care for his own self is always a public foe.

Of course the workman in any useful calling who reflects that his work is a social function will find in that fact a motive to do good work. Good bricklaying, good cotton spinning, good plumbing, not only bring the workmen wages; they increase the comfort and the welfare of those who enjoy the product. The beneficence of the work is a motive to which we may wisely make appeal. Men will put love into their work if we only teach them that every honest work ought to be a labor of love. We have taught them so diligently the other thing for so many years that they have mainly lost sight of this inspiring motive. The day will come when we shall have here upon the earth a real chivalry of labor, workers of all ranks and callings who love to work not merely for the stipend, but also for the joy of service.

As we rise to the services that call for higher intelligence do we not find this motive entering still more consciously into our work? Here is the engineer taxing his imagination, summoning his scholarship, marshaling his constructive powers to span the mighty river with the bridge of iron. What should be his motives? Should he be wholly intent upon the fee or upon the fame of his achievement? Doubtless he will think of both these things; but may we not also believe that some sense of the value of this work to his fellow men would add inspiration and energy to his efforts? Here are two cities to be brought into

closer neighborhood; the great army of
toilers will pass from one to the other more
quickly and more securely; fatigue will be
lessened, danger will be averted for a
great multitude; nay, the East and the
West will be nearer together than they
were before, and the cruel distance that
divides loving hearts will be shortened,
though it be ever so little. How greatly
the sum of human comfort and welfare will
be increased by this structure! And now
shall the man who plans it and builds it
shut all these thoughts out of his mind?
Shall he think only of how his personal
fortune will be advanced by the success of
the enterprise? No; it is not necessary to
degrade our work to this mean level. We
are not really so base as this, and it is not
possible that our economists should per-
suade us that we are. The engineer will
be no sentimentalist if he say to himself:
"I will build this bridge wisely and well.

There shall be no defect in the construction
that my vigilance can provide against, no
weakness that art and patience can remove. It shall stand for many a day after
I am gone, and the millions who intrust
themselves to it shall believe that they are
safe, and shall have reason for their confidence. It shall shorten the journey of
many weary feet; it shall bring the ends of
the earth a little nearer together; it shall
hasten in some small measure the day
when there shall be no more barriers
between city and city and nation and
nation, when mankind shall be one brotherhood."

So the architect who builds the home
or the school, the temple or the capitol,
may well consider that the structures
which he is rearing will not only add to the
comfort and happiness of those who shall
inhabit and use them, but shall also stand
when he is silent, enforcing the gospel of

strength and beauty upon all who pass by
—street preachers of a true ordination and
a beneficent ministry. The value of his
work not only in increasing the world's
resources of shelter and of comfort, but
also in educating the tastes of men and in
lifting up their thoughts, ought to be appar-
ent to him, and ought to furnish a good
part of his inspiration.

Is it possible that work which touches
the happiness and welfare of society so
nearly should be rightly done by one who
never thinks of this larger result? When a
man's work does link him so closely with
his fellow men, is it rational that he should
remain in stolid indifference to the fact?
Will not his work be nobler work, happier
work, if he keep this motive always within
the horizon of his thought? And will not
the community in which this motive is
emphasized and obeyed be a happier community than the one in which each indi-

vidual is taught that it is his one big duty
to take care of his own self?

Let it not be imagined that this spirit
finds expression in the constructive industries alone. It belongs just as truly to
the life of the merchant, of the professional
man, of the organizer of labor, as to the
life of the mechanic and engineer and the
architect. The merchant—is not he, too,
serving his fellow men? The work of exchange, when honorably conducted, only
reënforces and completes the work of production. Commerce is the handmaid of
industry. It is the merchant's business
to furnish to his fellow men the goods
necessary for their life and happiness.
For this they give him some recompense,
as is meet; but is he never to think of
the beneficence of his work and of how he
can make it even more serviceable to his
fellow men? Must he confine his thoughts
to his profits? Is there nothing in this

calling of his but the gain he can make out of it?

"Observe," says Mr. Ruskin, "the merchant's function is to provide for the nation. It is no more his function to get profit for himself out of that provision than it is a clergyman's function to get his stipend. The stipend is a due and necessary adjunct, but not the object of his life, if he be a true clergyman, any more than his fee (or honorarium) is the object of his life to a true physician. Neither is his profits the object of life to a true merchant. All these, if true men, have a work to be done irrespective of fee; the pastor's function being to teach, the physician's to heal, and the merchant's, as I have said, to provide. That is to say, he has to understand to their very root the qualities of the thing he deals in, and the means of obtaining or producing it; and he has to apply all his sagacity and energy to the producing or obtaining it in perfect state, and distributing it at the cheapest possible price when it is most needed."[1]

Hear, O shopkeeper! Is this your calling? Is not this the very work you are called to do? Not merely to get from your customers as many as you can of their dimes and dollars; not merely to make the largest possible profit out of the wares you sell, but also to minister industriously, sagaciously, wisely, to their needs. Not, as we have seen already, to be a vender of poison or destruction of any sort—you are not called to that! Not to supply all demands, but only those that make for life and happiness. People may wish you to furnish them the means of committing physical or moral suicide in a more or less expeditious fashion; they may offer to make it profitable for you to do so, but you will not do it, if you know it. You will study

[1] Unto this Last, p. 39.

to make your calling nobly serviceable to your fellow men; and when that motive stands confessed and shapes your service your counter may be, as George Macdonald says, an altar, and your trade a sacrament.

Mr. Ruskin, in the passage which I quoted, includes the manufacturer in the mercantile class. Hear what he says of the merchant as manufacturer:

"Because the production or obtaining of any commodity involves necessarily the agency of many lives and hands, the merchant becomes in the course of his business the master and the governor of large masses of men in a more direct though less confessed way than a military officer or pastor; so that on him falls, in great part, the responsibility for the kind of life they lead; and it becomes his duty not only to be always considering how to produce what he sells in the purest and cheapest forms, but how to make the various employments

be involved in the production or trans-
ference of it most beneficial to the men
employed."[1]

The social function of the organizer and
employer of labor is thus brought into
clear light. Not only is it his duty to
see that the work about which he keeps
them busy is work that ministers to the
welfare of society, it is also his duty to take
good care that the men themselves are not
hurt by it. He must study broadly the
effect of his enterprise on the community;
he must study closely and narrowly its
effect upon the workmen whom he has
called to aid him in it. It is this particular
section of society for which he is directly
responsible; this is his parish, and he must
not neglect it. He is making his fortune
out of the labor of these people; he must
not manage his business in such a way that
the workmen shall be degraded or weak-

[1] Ibid., p. 40.

ened or discouraged or embittered by it.
Society has loaned to him these men and
women for his profit; it expects him to de-
liver them up, or their natural successors,
when he is done with them, in good health,
in good heart, in good hope, worth as much
to society as when he took them.   That is
certainly a part, a very important part, of
his one big duty.   These people are affected
physically, mentally, morally, socially, for
good or ill, by the work they are doing for
him, by the conditions under which the
work is done, by the influences round about
them in their work, by his personal relation to them.   It is for him to choose that,
so far as he can compass it, they shall receive good and not ill in all this relation.
Let him not say, "I pay them their wages,
and there my duty ends."   It was Cain
who said that, or words to that effect.
And the curse of Cain will rest on any
man who, purposely or thoughtlessly,

suffers the manhood of his workmen to
be despoiled in the building of his fortunes.

I trust that these illustrations have
brought before your minds the nature of
that True Socialism for which this discourse is a plea—a Socialism that is not of
the letter, but of the spirit; that begins,
where all radical and beneficent reforms
begin, in the tempers and aims of men, and
shapes the social order not by an outward
pressure, but by an inward law. That
some readjustment of our industrial methods is necessary I do not doubt, but all
steps taken in that direction must be ten-
tative and slow. The great thing to be
done is not to reconstruct the social machinery, but, as a wise man has expressed
it, "to socialize the individual." The
thing to be got rid of is not the system
which puts on the individual the responsibility of self-support, but the philosophy

that makes the dog with his bone the type of the good citizen.

The True Socialism—what better words could be found to describe it than those of Mr. Henry Sidgwick, a great thinker and a great economist, when he confesses his feeling of "a moral need of some means of developing in the members of a modern industrial community a fuller consciousness of their industrial work as a social function, only rightly performed when done with a cordial regard to the welfare of the whole society"?

You see now where I got the text of this preachment; and it would be difficult to find among recent writers a better authority.

And I think you can perceive that the hearty recognition of the truth which we have been considering would give to our daily work, whatever it might be, a dignity and nobility that it often lacks. What is it that makes work drudgery—what but the spirit of him who cried, "Am I my brother's keeper? My one big duty is to care for my own self"? This spirit it was that loaded work with a curse at the beginning, and will to the end. That curse will never be lifted till men learn the new law that no man liveth to himself.

How the toiler's burden is lightened when he thinks, "This work of mine, done thoroughly, loyally, cheerfully, as I am doing it, will not only bring livelihood to me and those dear to me, it will help to swell the sum of comfort and delight for my fellow men; it will help to make the world a safer, roomier, pleasanter place to live in"! Is not this true of all honest work, and is it not the truth that every honest worker most needs to know? Of all true art this is the inspiration. What impulse to noble art could spring in the soul that cares for itself alone? The great builders

—are they, were they ever, men whose main care was for the architect's commission? The great painters—are they men who paint only for the market, pot-hunters in the fields of beauty? The great singers —is it pelf that prompts their songs? Nay; the dog with his bone is not a singer. All the impulses to the noblest art must arise from those broader thoughts and larger loves by which the man is made one with his kind. Your analysis of humanity into individuals kills art; it is only when the synthesis of humanity is fully realized that great art work is done.

What kind of world this would be if this impulse were universal, if it even came to be broadly influential in human life, recognized by all as a true motive, even though not fulfilled by all, I leave you to imagine. How quickly the feud of rich and poor would be quieted! How speedily these tough problems of our social life would be

solved! How easily we should exterminate
the parasites that suck the life out of our
industries and these plunderers that fatten
on the state! Bright vision it is, and we
must not put it too far away from us!

> " For slow and sure comes up the golden year,
>   When wealth no more shall rest in mounded
>   heaps,
>   But smit with freer light shall slowly melt
>   In many streams to fatten lower lands;
>   And light shall spread, and man be liker man,
>   Through all the circle of the golden year."

To the young men and women, soon
going forth to the labors of life, I especially
intrust this great thought, not without
hope that they will find out what it means
and how to use it. Something they will
do, I know, to hasten the coming of that
golden year, when all men's good shall be
each man's rule; and they must not forget,
in the hours when its happy advent seems
very far off,

> " That unto him who works, and feels he works,
>   This same grand year is ever at the doors."

V
Lights and Shadows of Municipal Reform

IT is now about ten or twelve years since
the problem of municipal reform began to
be a matter of serious consideration in the
United States. I do not mean to imply
that the subject had never been thought
of before that time; for many individuals,
here and there, had been giving it attention. The exposure of the operations of
the Tweed ring in New York, in the summer of 1871, made a profound impression
upon thinking people, yet most of us were
inclined to assume that such rascalities
were mainly confined to New York city
and to Tammany Hall.

In the seventies some anxiety began to
be felt in other quarters concerning municipal conditions; in 1874 a Citizens' Associa-

tion was formed in Chicago, whose object was "to insure a more perfect administration in our municipal affairs; to promote the general welfare and prosperity of the city; to protect citizens, so far as possible, from the effects of careless or corrupt legislation; to effect the prompt enforcement and execution of the law," with other purposes, economic and commercial, as well as civic. I do not know how much work was done by that association, but it had a name to live. In 1878 was formed in New York Dr. Parkhurst's famous Society for the Prevention of Crime. A Citizens' Association with aims similar to that of Chicago was formed in Albany in 1881; another in Boston in 1887; another in Buffalo in 1888. In Baltimore in 1885 the Reform League was organized; the Municipal Association of Philadelphia in 1886; and the Library Hall Association of Cambridge in 1889. I have thus named

eight organizations which had been formed
before the nineties in the interests of municipal reform. There were others, I am
sure; one in Saint Louis, if I mistake not.
But the early nineties witnessed a notable
uprising of the people of the cities in behalf
of better government. I have a sketch of
"Municipal Reform Movements," probably quite imperfect, printed in 1895; and
in that I find the names and constitutions
of three municipal reform associations organized in 1892, six in 1893, and twenty-
seven in 1894. This list covers the principal cities of the country, and includes the
Municipal Leagues of Philadelphia and
Boston, the Civic Federation of Chicago,
the City Club of New York, the Committee
of Public Safety in Saint Louis, and many
other strong associations. It will be seen
therefore that the efflorescence of this plant
occurred about a dozen years ago; it was
then that the subject of better government

for cities began to be vigorously agitated. The National Municipal League was formed in 1894, and its intelligent and vigorous agitation has contributed not a little to the spread of knowledge and the awakening of sound sentiment. Other national organizations have followed in its wake, among them the League of American Municipalities, consisting of the officers of city governments, who meet annually to discuss the problems of the city.

We have had, then, a little more than a decade of pretty vigorous discussion and agitation respecting the government of our cities; scores of volumes dealing with this subject have been published, several periodicals devoted to municipal reform have been established, and hundreds of pamphlets and magazine articles have appeared in which all phases of the question have been presented. A great deal of thought has been expended on municipal organiza-

tion; some, at least, of the states have
had commissions appointed to study the
subject and prepare laws or constitutional
amendments regulating the matter. The
National Municipal League has devoted
much time to this phase of the question,
and has submitted a model charter for the
guidance of municipalities seeking improvements in their organic law.

What are the fruits of all this agitation?
How stands the matter to-day, after ten
years of debate and struggle? Have we
made any progress? Is there any better
outlook for good government in our cities
now than there was ten years ago? To this
question my own answer would be something like that of the old prophet to whom
the challenge came, "Watchman, what of
the night?" and whose oracular reply was,
"The morning cometh, and also the night."
Dawn was in sight, but darkness was falling
fast. There were signs of hope and of dis-

couragement. Light and shadow were contending for the mastery. Such is the situation of our municipal problem as it presents itself to my own mind.

It is better, perhaps, to look at the dark side first, and gather up the more promising aspects later for the invigoration of our hope.

It must be owned that the last decade has witnessed some of the worst developments that have ever appeared in American municipalities. Perhaps the gigantic robberies of the Tweed ring were bolder and more flagrant than any which have followed them. Simon Sterne tells us that in the year 1870 the leading officers of New York took directly from the city treasury, by raised bills, not less than $15,000,000; and that the entire amount they fraudulently appropriated was not less than $25,000,000. Recent operations have been of a very different character. No city administration which has existed during the past ten years would have dared to attempt such a direct raid upon the treasury. A good many severe things have been said about Tammany under Croker's reign, but Croker's Tammany never pillaged the city treasury to any alarming extent; that was not Croker's way. The greatest villainies of the decade just past have been perpetuated by other methods than those of Tweed; they have consisted sometimes in using the power of the city to levy blackmail upon all sorts and conditions of people for the benefit of those in office, and sometimes in the corrupt granting of franchises, by which strong corporations were given power to bleed the people for their own aggrandizement.

Nobody will ever know how much money Croker's Tammany took out of the pockets of the people of New York. It was levied largely on the predatory classes, on

the liquor sellers and the gamblers and the
keepers of vile houses, who had to pay
heavily for immunity. But Tammany was
no respecter of persons; its tribute was
exacted from the evil and the good, the
just and the unjust; the corporations that
wanted franchises had to pay for them,
and every merchant and every householder
was liable to be threatened with annoy-
ances or injuries of one kind or another
against which he could protect himself only
by the payment to the police of some
tribute, large or small. Never, I suppose,
was highway robbery either reduced to so
fine an art or raised to such gigantic pro-
portions as under the reign of Richard the
Good in Gotham. The worst of it is that
the system of blackmail seems to have become so firmly rooted in this great metrop-
olis that it is now very difficult to extirpate
it; that is the task which Mr. Low was not
quite able to accomplish, and which is

giving Mr. McClellan and Mr. McAdoo a great deal of trouble.

Perhaps the most discouraging aspect of our municipal problem at the present moment is what we are wont to call the moral problem—the difficulty of preserving order and decency, the difficulty of controlling vice and shameful iniquity. My belief is that there are few of the larger cities in which the conditions in this respect are not worse than they were ten years ago. My impressions on this subject may be incorrect—I hope that they are—but what I have seen and heard makes me believe that there is less restraint upon the more flagrant forms of vice in most of our cities at the present day than there was ten years ago; that all-night drinking places are more common; that gambling places are more numerous and more openly plying their traffic; that "ladies' parlors," and all such unspeakable devices by which the young are entrapped and destroyed, flourish with less notice from the police; that prostitution is more shameless and more ubiquitous than ever before. All this indicates a prevailing rottenness in the police departments of our cities. My own belief is that it results largely from the manner in which we have dealt with the liquor question.

The laws and ordinances by which we have undertaken to regulate the sale of liquor have been laws and ordinances which could not be enforced in our cities. We may lay down this proposition: that a law is not a good law for any republican community if more than half the people of that community honestly think it a bad law and intend to disobey it if they can. No matter how perfect it may be according to ideal standards, it is a thoroughly bad law if the majority of the people of the community conscientiously disapprove of it, and regard it as oppressive and injurious

to them. If such is their attitude toward it
they will not help to enforce it; it is more
probable that they will habitually disobey
it. It is true that if they were ideal citizens
they would respect and uphold the law
because it is law, until it is repealed, pre-
ferring to suffer the injury which it inflicts
on them rather than weaken the force of
all law by openly disobeying it; but they
are not all ideal citizens, and very few of
them will take this high ground. The law
will, therefore, be habitually disobeyed by
a majority of the people. Such a law cannot be enforced by the police. It is impossible for a minority of the people even
with the aid of the police, to impose their
will upon the majority of the people.

The police authorities in dealing with a
situation of this kind become thoroughly
demoralized. They learn to play fast and
loose with their obligations; all their ideas
about the sacredness of law are debauched;

they come to feel that their own discretion is their only guide in the enforcement of laws. This is the history of the relation of our police authorities to liquor legislation. The liquor laws, as a rule, have been laws which the majority of the people of our larger cities honestly believe to be unjust and oppressive, and therefore they habitually violate them. Doubtless their ideals ought to be higher, but they are what they are, and we shall never raise them by force of law. We cannot lift up their standards by force, but they can drag ours down by force. The law itself, by which we attempt to coerce them, suffers mortally through their hatred for it and contempt of it; all law is dishonored and degraded. The men who are charged with its administration are the first to feel this, and the result is that their moral standards are blurred and debased, and their attitude toward law-breakers of all classes becomes ambiguous if not thoroughly false. To the keepers of gambling houses and brothels the same immunity is extended as the keepers of drinking places have secured, and thus a kind of dry rot affect the whole police administration; it sometimes appears to exist not for the suppression but for the protection and promotion of vice and disorder.

It hardly needs to be said that these are precisely the conditions which favor the development of blackmailing as a business. Given the existence of a law which the community does not seriously expect to see enforced, and unscrupulous or mercenary police officials have the game in their own hands. The law is a good enough club to threaten with; they can use it to extort tribute, and when the law is not enforced nobody is greatly troubled. They can collect their hush money, save themselves the trouble of enforcing the law, and

escape severe censure because of their failure. It would be infinitely better to have
no law at all dealing with these vices than
to have them dealt with after the manner
which prevails in most of our cities.

It must be admitted, then, that one of
the darkest of the shadows resting on our
present field of observation is that which
is cast by the inefficiency and viciousness
of our methods of dealing with social vice.
I fear that the area and the density of this
shadow is increasing, and there is a loud
call for serious thought upon the problem
which it presents.

The shadow which lies next to this is
that which is produced by corrupt relations between public service corporations
and city governments. I suppose that
there are still a good many of our smaller
cities which are yet comparatively free
from this curse. I am told that in my old
home, Springfield, Massachusetts, there

has never been any suspicion of a job; that the city's business has been done, thus far, intelligently and honestly in the interest of the people; and when I read that the street car lines—a splendid system—are capitalized for only a little over $30,000 a mile, while the average capitalization of street railways in the Central States in 1897 was $91,000 a mile, and of the Middle States $128,000 a mile, I am inclined to think that there must be some truth in the claim. Of course, there are other cities where the public interests are cared for intelligently and faithfully, and where promoters have not been permitted to fatten upon the tribute wrung by law from the toiling multitude. But those deadly averages which I just quoted forbid us to entertain any very complacent beliefs about the prevailing conditions. The figures abundantly show that public service companies, street car lines, gas and electric lighting companies, and all such, are capitalized as a rule for from two to four times the cost of their plants, which means, of course, that the people are compelled to pay two to four times as much interest on this capital as they ought to pay; which also means that city governments have been so ignorant or so corrupt as to make contracts with these companies by which this tribute has been levied upon the people.   In many cases this has been due to ignorance, to a wholly inadequate comprehension of the value of the franchises given away; but in many other cases it has been done with a knowledge which, if not adequate, was at least sufficient to secure for the corrupt officials considerable plunder.   I have no idea, for my part, that the venal city officials ever get for their votes anything like what they are worth to the people who buy them.   Probably for every thousand that the companies have spent

in bribing they have got a million of ex-
cessive profit; such venal officials are, as a
rule, a cheap lot.

Operations of this nature have been
scandalously common during the past ten
years. The lease of the gas works in Philadelphia by the Councils of that city to a
great gas syndicate is one of the most
notorious instances of this alliance between city officials and public service corporations. Here was a franchise granting
to a company the right to supply the city
with gas for a term of years at a certain
rate; and while the contract was pending
another perfectly reputable and responsible company offered to give the city
$9,000,000 for the privilege of rendering
the same service, for the same length of
time, at the same rate. Was the question
debated? Hardly, I think, by those who
proposed to refuse this offer. It was not a
debatable question, you see; the only rule

to apply to it was the old rule of "addi-
tion, division, and silence." These councilmen were, probably, very philanthropic
men, and they did not like to let their left
hands know what their right hands were
doing.

The newspapers of Philadelphia, the
people, almost with one voice, cried out
against this robbery; besought, clamored,
demanded that the question be submitted
to a popular vote. One of the newspapers
had a referendum vote taken, with ballot
boxes and printed ballots, in one of the
wards, and the vote was 32 in favor of the
granting of the franchise and 2,583 against
it. That fairly represented the popular
wish, and the Councils knew it; but the
franchise was granted. This is the story
of the way the Philadelphia city officials,
in the words of the Hon. Wayne MacVeagh,
were "bribed by the rich to rob the poor."
No bribery in this instance was brought

home to anybody; how much it cost this
corporation to get its lease of the gas
works we shall never know. It is not im-
probable that the corporation got several
votes for nothing; other great corporations
friendly to it may have owned some of
these councilmen and may have forced
their henchmen to do their bidding. And
it is equally probable that others were controlled in the same way by certain bosses
at a comparatively small expense to the
corporation.

So successful was this operation that
when the Traction Company in the same
city afterward wished to obtain a new
franchise the city officials scarcely hesi-
tated to give what was demanded; and
when John Wanamaker sent a letter to
the mayor offering $2,500,000 for the fran-
chise which the city was parting with for
nothing, the mayor, suspecting the con-
tents of the letter, threw it unopened into

the waste-basket. That is the way they do things in Philadelphia.

Stories like this can be read by no man of character and conscience without a sinking of the heart. How can such things be? Is there no public conscience, no sense of honor or decency, no power to resist robbery and oppression? The blackest of the shadows which appear upon the municipal landscape is the apathy with which communities of American men stand and look on while such things are being done, meekly permitting the corporations and the city officials to bind heavy burdens upon them which they will be compelled to carry for generations.

Many other communities, large and small, have suffered in this same way. For an instance of the way they do it in smaller towns a friend, whose home is in Orange, New Jersey, told me of an experience with the City Council of that small municipality a few years ago. The street railway was asking for an extension of its lines, and the people thought that in exchange for this grant the railway ought to make some important concessions to the public. Accordingly they investigated the matter carefully, and a large delegation of the most intelligent citizens went before the Council and proved, by the experience of other cities, that the railway could well afford to reduce fares and give transfers. The argument was complete; nobody attempted to call it in question; but without debate the Council stolidly sat still and voted the franchise exactly as the railway wanted it.

I read a similar story about a subway in Syracuse. The mayor had proved to the Council that the city ought to receive a considerable sum for this grant; but the majority of the Council, without trying to reply to his arguments, gave it to the company for nothing.

A more flagrant case was the passage of an ordinance by the Indianapolis Council giving to the street railway company of that city a franchise running thirty-five years, for which, I dare say, shrewd capitalists would have been willing to give a great many millions of dollars. This measure was rushed through the City Council in less than twenty-four hours from the time of its introduction, all the newspapers in the city advocating it. Such expedition and such unanimity are certainly phenomenal.

I am only giving a few samples of the kind of thing which has been going on during the past ten years in all parts of the country. By such combinations of public service corporations with venal city officials burdens amounting to hundreds of millions of dollars have been bound about the necks of the people of our cities.

I do not need to refer to the recent astounding developments in Saint Louis

and in Minneapolis and in Grand Rapids.
The shadows have been lying heavily all
over those fair cities. The rottenness there
uncovered is the most flagrant, the most
astounding, that has come to light since
the exposure of the Tweed ring.

Only one more serious discouragement
will I mention—one which affects only my
own state. We were confronted two years
ago with an emergency in Ohio which
compelled the calling of the Legislature to
frame a new municipal code for the government of all our cities. It was a great opportunity. We might have availed ourselves of the world's best experience and
secured for ourselves an organic frame-
work for municipalities which would have
been favorable to efficient government. It
is quite true that the best governmental
machinery in the world will not guarantee
good government unless the people choose
good men to administer it, and watch them

and support them in the administration;
but some kinds of municipal machinery
are better than others, and we might, if
we had been intelligent and patriotic
enough, have got the best for Ohio. Instead of that we have got a very clumsy,
inefficient, ill-contrived apparatus, which
is sure to discourage good men from undertaking official responsibilities, to cripple
all endeavors after unity and coherency of
administration, and to give us a great deal
of trouble before we are done with it.
The cause of municipal reform in Ohio
might have been materially advanced by
the action of our Legislature; instead of
that it has suffered a very serious reverse.

The tendency in all recent municipal
organization has been to concentrate the
executive power in the mayor—following
the analogy of our national government.
The tendency is a good one provided due
regard is paid to the legislative branch of

the government and the Council is given
power which fairly belongs to it. For administration a centralized executive seems
to be in the line of all business experience.
Nobody supposes that the business at
Washington would be better done if the
Army Department and the Navy Department and the Interior Department and the
Post Office Department and the Treasury
Department were each of them under the
control of a commission of three or five
men elected by the people, over whom the
President had no control. In cities, not
less than in the national government, there
is need of unity of administration, and it
is best secured by the concentration of executive responsibility in the mayor. But
we in Ohio have repudiated this principle,
taking away from the mayor nearly all
control of the great business departments
of the city, putting all these under a board
of public service consisting of three or five

members to be elected every two years by
the people. Over all these departments
including the streets, the sewers, the docks,
the levees, the public buildings, the mar-
kets, the parks, the waterworks, the lighting, the mayor has no longer any control;
the board of public service is supreme,
organizing its own subdepartments, fixing
salaries, appointing and dismissing its own
employees, with no other civil service regu-
lations than those which it chooses to estab-
lish and enforce. It is an astonishing
fabrication, and it illustrates the baneful
and paralyzing influence of state politics
upon municipal affairs.

I have succeeded, I am sure, in this
rough sketch, in bringing to your minds the
truth which is too familiar to all of us, that
American cities, after all our agitation
and discussion, are still, as a rule, in a
very unsatisfactory condition. There is
no single thing of which Americans have

so great reason to be ashamed as of the manner in which their cities are governed. The one thing of which Americans are most apt to boast is their government, but the most important branch of government is that of our municipalities; that touches our interests far more nearly, affects our characters more deeply, concerns our welfare more vitally, than does the government of the state or the nation, and at this most critical point of all we are making a miserable and disastrous failure. That is the indubitable and humiliating fact, and it is well for us to face it.

There are, however, other aspects of this subject which we must not fail to see. The shadows are black enough, but there are gleams of light.

First, we must not forget that some significant victories have been won for good government during the last decade. Our greatest city has witnessed some of the

most significant and decisive of these.
The fight in New York is perhaps more
desperate than in any other city, (1) because the sediment of immigration settles
there, the class of immigrants making
their way to the interior being as a rule
more intelligent and more enterprising
than those who stay in New York; (2) because so large a portion of those doing
business in the city are nonresidents, living
in New Jersey and in the northern suburbs;
and (3) because a corrupt power has been
intrenched there so many years.   In spite
of these great difficulties great gains have
been made in New York within the last
ten years.   Twice the city has been carried
by the forces of reform; and this is an
achievement which ought to give heart to
men of good will in all American cities.
If New York can elect by popular vote
such men as Mayor Strong and Mayor Low,
with such tremendous party odds against

them; if such people as the dwellers on the East Side can be persuaded to cast their votes in the interest of clean politics, no city needs to despair.

The administration of Mayor Strong was a great improvement over those which preceded it, and some gains were made which will never be wholly lost. The street cleaning under Waring was a historic achievement; New York will never relapse into the condition out of which he raised it. A great deal was done also toward the abatement of the slums and the provision of parks and playgrounds, of which Mr. Riis has told us so eloquently.

It is not necessary to review in this place the municipal history of New York; it is familiar enough to many of you. But it is certain that municipal conditions there are vastly better than they were ten years ago. The election of Mr. Low and Mr. Jerome was a notable victory, and standards of honesty and efficiency were again lifted which are not likely to be permanently lowered. Mr. Low was defeated, but he was defeated by a capable and honorable man. None other could have defeated him, and he himself had made it necessary that such a man should be pitted against him. The present administration, which seems to those who look on from a distance to be doing reasonably well, is part of the fruit of the victory that was won when Mr. Low and Mr. Jerome were elected. Its weakest point seems to be the police department, and that was the greatest failure of Mr. Low's administration. It is apt, as I have said, to be the weak point in municipal governments everywhere. But on the whole municipal conditions in New York are a great deal better than they were ten years ago.

In Chicago, also, hopeful signs are vis-

ible. The steady improvement of the
Chicago City Council is the most striking
fact, perhaps, in the whole field of view.
In our American city governments the
Council has almost always been the weakest point; we have often succeeded in
electing respectable mayors, but the Councils elected with them have generally been
made up of very inferior material. Twenty-
five or thirty years ago men of character
and substance were often found in City
Councils; the quality, in recent years, in
most cities, has been steadily and grievously deteriorating. Yet this is the point
of greatest danger. The legislative branch
of our city government holds the purse,
makes contracts, and grants franchises to
public service corporations. It is here
that corruption nests and breeds. Weak
or unprincipled men in the Council become the tools of conscienceless manipu-
lators of capital, and aid them in binding

heavy burdens upon the people of the cities. The ablest and most upright men in the cities ought to be in the City Councils. To intrust such vast interests to men who are destitute of intelligence, of business experience, and character is little short of idiocy. Such men can be easily bamboozled or bribed by the shrewd lawyers or the rascally promoters who represent the great corporations.

Some sense of the importance of this branch of the government seems to have taken possession of the minds of the people of Chicago, for, according to all reports the Council of that city has been steadily rising in capacity and in character, until it has come to be a better legislative body than any other of our greater cities can boast. For the last year or two the question of a new franchise for the traction interests of Chicago has been before that body, and although hundreds of millions of dollars are involved, it has not been possible to carry through the Council any corrupt scheme. The matter, which is a very difficult one, is still in suspense, but the prospect is that the interests of the people will be fully protected.

The method by which this result—the improvement of the character of the Council—has been secured is not less noteworthy than the result itself. That a few men, a very few men, only seven, I think, of clear veracity, of undoubted integrity, free from all suspicion of partisanship, should be able by carefully investigating the record of every candidate and telling the whole truth about him, without fear or favor, to influence the votes of so many of their fellow citizens is a most encouraging phenomenon. It should greatly reassure those who are inclined to lose faith in democracy. Clear and fearless truth-telling on the part of men who have won the confidence of their fellow citizens is a mighty weapon in this campaign.

Other signs are not less reassuring. The Herculean achievements of Mr. Folk in Saint Louis, and the fact that he has been rewarded for his courage and virtue by the elevation to the governorship of the state, where his control of the situation in the city is assured—all this is a splendid victory for good municipal government. And in Minneapolis a triumph not less signal has been won by the recent election to the mayoralty of one of the strongest and noblest of the young men of that city.

A novel incident in this warfare is also reported from Los Angeles. The charter of that city permits the people to remove from office inefficient or corrupt officials. On a petition, signed by one third of those who voted in the preceding election, the City Council is required to order a new election; and under this law an alderman who was believed to be acting corruptly was required to submit his claim to the voters who had chosen him. By a large majority he was removed from office, and a better man was put in his place. This is the first instance of the kind, I believe, in the history of this country. It suggests a method which may yet be effectively used in improving democratic government. [1]

These are omens for good. They show us that the problem is not unsolvable; that if we will put our wits and our energy and our resolution into the business we may have as good city government in America as they have in England or Germany. We could find many more such encourag-

[1] It seems something less than just to reduce to a footnote the remarkable revolution which has taken place in Philadelphia during the present year. Nothing more encouraging has appeared in the recent history of American cities. No more striking demonstration of the irresistible power of a sound public opinion has ever been witnessed.

ing signs if we could make ourselves familiar with the recent municipal history of
our American cities. My own impression
is that recent contracts with public service
companies have generally been far more
favorable to the people than those of
earlier date. The people are becoming
aware of the enormous value of these
franchises, and it will soon be difficult to
perpetrate such robberies as have been
common in the past.

Of all the indications of a better day
the one most cheering is the deepening
sense of responsibility for good government
on the part of the citizens of sense and
substance. Such a generalization as this
is somewhat unsafe; few men have knowledge enough of all our urban communities to warrant them in any positive
statement concerning the general movements of public opinion in them. I only
give my own impression—that the people

of the cities are beginning to have a little more conviction of sin, and to ask more earnestly what they must do to be saved.

In the earlier stages of this agitation the notion was prevalent that some new and improved municipal machinery was the one thing needful—a revision of the charter, new powers given to somebody or new restrictions placed on somebody else; but we have found out, some of us, that the best methods in the world will fail to give us good government if they are operated by bad men.   In fact—and this is a truth which I want to emphasize—the more efficient the governmental machinery is, the better it is adapted to its legitimate purpose in the hands of the men who ought to run it, the more mischief will be done with it if we put it in the hands of unprincipled and selfish men.   The initiative, the executive power and responsibility, that a good man *must have* to make his administration effective, enables a bad man to do a vast amount of injury. Not a few cities which have exhausted their civic enthusiasm in securing reformed and improved charters, and then have permitted the offices to be filled by incapable and corrupt men, have had rather worse government under the new machinery than they had under the old. And there are a great many people in all these cities who are now of the opinion that the worse government under which they are suffering is due to the new methods, and who are clamoring to go back to the old ways. But there is still a remnant, I think, in most cities, who have a little common sense, and who are able, by this time, to see that while good methods are better than bad methods in the hands of good men, the best methods are not only useless but even mischievous in the hands of bad men; that the one essential thing is to find

capable and upright officials and put the
power into their hands and *leave it there;*
and that this can never be looked for
until in the hearts of the people themselves there is a spirit of service and a
spirit of sacrifice—a recognition of the
priceless value of good municipal government and a willingness to take the time
and put forth the effort and make the
sacrifice which are needed to secure it.
You cannot get good, competent, honest,
unselfish municipal government out of a
greedy, rapacious, selfish, money-grubbing
community. You cannot get good city
government out of a community which
cares more for "business" than for anything else. Men who have no time and
no thought for anything but their own
interests, who will never take any public
responsibilities, or bear any public burdens, *ought to be represented in the public
offices by men of no conscience and no*

thought for anything but their own interests —and they always will be. This is the truth which is beginning to dawn upon a good many of the people of this time, and the entrance of this idea into the heads of our business men will give us more light on this question than anything else that I can think of.

Let us dwell a little before we separate from this phase of our subject. There is a principle here involved which it may be well for us to get well lodged in our own minds. That is the principle of reciprocity which rules, whether we will or no, in all our social relations; which in every social relation forbids men to be receivers only and not givers; which requires every man in every social relation to give as freely as he receives. It is not merely true that we ought to do this; it is true that we must do it, or take the consequences.

Even in the economic realm we see this

principle at work.   The agriculturist must
not ask his land to give him crops, year
by year, without rendering to it any return for its bounty.   If you want your soil
to be liberal you must make it fat.   The
product of the soil must in some measure
be returned to the soil, or some equivalent
for it, if its fruitfulness is to continue.

There are farmers who skin their land
by constant cropping and no fertilizing,
but it is ruinous economy for the owner
and a grave wrong to the community;
for whoever reduces the wealth of the
nation's soil and the sources of the supply
of sustenance is guilty of unsocial conduct.

In like manner the selfish tendency of
the capitalistic classes to reduce as much
as they can the laborers' share of the
common product tends, in the most pal-
pable manner, to the impoverishment of
all.   The farmers who skin their land and
the capitalists who skin their laborers are

engaged in an equally senseless business.
If the laborers are so poor that they can
buy but little, then little is sold and little
can be manufactured, and merchants and
bankers fail and mill wheels stop and rail-
roads go into receivers' hands and there
is general depression. The capital that
wants the lion's share gets the donkey's
share—and deserves it. If you wish to
live you must let live. If capital deserves
to prosper capital must help labor to be
prosperous; the contrary policy is not
merely bad, it is stupid.

Ascending to higher interests, we find
this relation of reciprocity subsisting between the citizens and their government.
The government of a republic is simply
that organization of institutions and services by means of which the people secure
for themselves protection against injury
and peril, the definition and regulation
of their common rights and interests, and

promotion of their common welfare. It
is a great coöperative enterprise in which
certain persons are selected to perform for
all the rest certain important services.
These officers of the state guard our fron-
tiers, protect our homes, define and maintain our rights of possession, run on our
errands, and carry our messages across
the continents and around the globe, keep
the peace between our nation and other
nations, and in a great many other ways
provide for wants that are common to all
the citizens. Of course it is important
that all this work be wisely organized and
faithfully administered; we all have an
interest in good government. But there
be many who are more than willing to
reap all the benefits of good government
without rendering any adequate return
therefor. A great many, indeed, there are
to whom the government is mainly a city
to be sacked or a palace to be looted. To

get their living out of the public treasury
and to make the service rendered therefor
as nearly as possible a sinecure is the chief
end of many unworthy citizens. There
are not a few whose main reason for wishing to obtain office is their confident expectation that they will get from the
state a far larger remuneration than they
ever could win in any private calling. Not
to serve the state but to fatten upon the
state is their ambition. I am not saying
that all men who hold office so regard it;
if anything like that were true the day of
doom would already have arrived; I am
saying that there are too many of this
class.

But it is not of these to whom office is
spoil that I am thinking so much as of
those who never hold office; of the great
body of private citizens who want to get
all the benefits of good government, but
who are not so ready as they ought to be

to make adequate returns for what they receive. They are even inclined, sometimes, to evade their share of the expense of the government by hiding their property, or making false returns, or wheedling or bribing the assessor. Not only this; they seek to avoid, so far as they can, public responsibilities and duties. They will not aid in securing honest and capable officials; they leave all the practical administration of government to those who make a business of politics. They want all the benefits of good government—adequate protection, faithful and efficient service—but they do not want to take the pains necessary to provide them. They intend to take out of the common fund their share, but do not intend to contribute to it their share.

Now, it should be evident that it is no more senseless policy for the farmer to skin the land or for the capitalist to skin

the laborer than it is for the citizen to skin
that great coöperative institution which
we call the state. The government of the
commonwealth will have just as much
fidelity and efficiency as we, the people, put
into it, and it can have no more. The
account is strictly kept, by the powers
that shape our ends, between the government and its citizens, and it is quite impossible for them to draw so heavily upon
it as most of them are inclined to do unless
they make constant contributions to its
fund of moral power and righteous purpose. The current here must flow both
ways. If the outward stream of public
administration is to be strong and pure,
the inward stream of patriotic thought
and unselfish service must be deep and
unfailing. They who are governed must
communicate to the powers that govern
them in all good things.

This is the general law, the law of reci-

procity. Let us bring it down to a nar-
rower application. The municipality quite
as obviously as the nation must come under it. The question of the city is the most
urgent of our social questions, and the
malady of the city is this very lack of reciprocity between the city and the citizen—
between that institution which we call the
municipality and those who live under it
and profit by it.

All of us who live in cities or do business
of any kind in cities are deeply interested
in good city government. It is our interest
that life and property should be secure;
that disorders of all kinds should be re-
pressed; that the health of the city should
be preserved; that there should be good
streets, good water, good sewerage, good
lighting and transportation facilities, good
schools and libraries, good parks and
playgrounds and public baths, and that
all these should be furnished at a reasona-

ble cost; and there is not the slightest
reason why the people of a large city, coöperating for all these purposes, should not
get all these goods of life at a very low cost
—at a cost far lower than we ever do get
them here in America. There is not the
slightest reason, I say, why the dwellers
in a city may not enjoy all these great bless-
ings provided only that the municipality
be wisely organized and honestly administered. The business of organizing and
administering this government and of
maintaining high standards of purity and
efficiency in connection with it is the business of the citizens. It is their city; it is
their government; they and nobody else in
the world are responsible for it. Yet we
find them, in the very large majority of
cases, eager to get all the benefit they can
out of the municipality and apparently
determined to give as little as they can of
money and time and thought and courage

and faith and love to the maintenance of the civic life. They want this fountain of municipal ministry to their welfare to flow pure and strong through all their lives, but they do not propose to take any care about replenishing its sources. A good many of them, I fear, seek to evade financial responsibility for the maintenance of this work; through their neglect the municipal administration becomes so corrupt that its burdens are oppressive; and then those who have suffered it to become corrupt justify themselves on account of its corruption in shirking its burdens. But even those who are fairly honest in their returns to the assessor often refuse to take any further responsibility. They vote, generally, for such candidates as the gods of the caucus vouchsafe to send them, but that is all that they are willing to do. How, I wonder, do they conceive that the fund of patriotic purpose, of honorable

ambition, of high and unselfish regard for
the common weal, out of which all good
government must come, is to be kept full
for the service of all? What do they imagine to be the motive power of good
government? Is it money—the money
contributed by the taxpayers? Does anybody imagine that clean, just, honorable,
beneficent administration of municipal
affairs can be purchased with money?
No; there must be some higher and better motive power than that behind the
municipal government, or you will have
nothing but corruption and oppression.
There must be honesty that no bribe
would dare solicit, courage that quails not
before the onset of greed and passion, high-
mindedness that will not stoop to trickery
or chicane, fidelity to duty that takes no
thought for ease or pleasure, and an en-
thusiastic devotion to the public welfare
by which all selfish interests are sub-

merged. All this must be there in the minds and hearts of the men who are administering the government; all this high thought, strong purpose, and patriotic feeling must be in the very atmosphere of the public offices, or you cannot have good government. Who is to fill these offices with this atmosphere and the minds and hearts of these officials with these sentiments and thoughts and purposes? It is we the people who must do it. There is nobody else to whom we can look. And this is our primary duty—to create such a state of public opinion that the men whom we call to serve us will be compelled to take this view of their public duty. And this means a great deal. It means that we must make these interests of municipal government matters of the deepest interest to ourselves; it means that we must put love and faith and heroic resolve and consecrated endeavor into this business of governing the city, which is our highest business; it means that we must be ready, whenever we are summoned, to deny ourselves and take up the cross and give to it toilsome days and wakeful nights; it means that government of the people and for the people must be government by the people, and not by a boss or a machine. In short, if the people want good government to come out of the City Hall they must put intelligence, honesty, unselfishness, and honor into the City Hall, and keep them there. They must not expect the currents of righteous and benign administration to flow out of that reservoir unless currents of sound thinking and high endeavor are steadily flowing into it from the hearts and the homes of the people.

A city, even more obviously than a state, is a great coöperative association. Its compact population, its common conveniences. its facilities of intercourse and

interchange and communication connote
a vast amount of social capital which the
wise and enterprising may use for their own
profit and for the common good. But this
splendid opportunity depends on the maintenance of honest and efficient municipal
government. Let the administration become corrupt, and at once the burdens
that are laid on industry and enterprise
become too heavy to be borne; taxes and
assessments eat up all the profits of business; rents are consumed by public charges,
and no man can afford to own the house
he lives in. Thus the benefits arising from
life in the city are practically canceled by
municipal maladministration; what ought
to be a great advantage to all becomes a
doubtful good if not a source of injury.
But all this arises from the habit of the
citizens of seeking to get all the benefit they
can out of it while they ignore the obligation to keep the municipal life sound and

sweet and pure by the contribution to it of honest effort and unselfish service. What they are trying to do is to skin the city, as the foolish farmer skins his land, and the result is not dissimilar.

I trust that we have succeeded in getting before our minds that relation of reciprocity which individuals sustain to the institutions in and by means of which they live and move and have their being. A large part of our lives is involved in the life of these institutions; their infirmity is our impoverishment; their failure is our destruction. If through our neglect they are weakened the injury falls directly upon ourselves. Upon the health and vigor of the civic life all we who dwell in cities or prosecute our callings in them must depend for our welfare, and the health and vigor of our civic life depend on our contributions of sound thinking, courageous speaking, consecrated service. If the king-

dom of heaven ever comes to your city it
will come in and through the City Hall;
that is the place where it will first be visible; but its origin will be in the hearts of
citizens to whom public good is no less
dear than private gain.